IN VITAL Harmony

CHARLOTTE MASON AND THE NATURAL LAWS OF EDUCATION

KAREN GLASS

www.karenglass.net

ISBN: 9781700769800

Typeset using the Merriweather font family:
www.sorkintype.com

Book Cover Design and Illustrations: Elizabeth Sage née Glass

We should hail a workable, effectual philosophy of education as a deliverance from much perplexity. Before this great deliverance comes to us it is probable that many tentative efforts will be put forth, having more or less of the characters of a philosophy; notably, having a central idea, a body of thought with various members working in vital harmony.
—Charlotte Mason—

This book is dedicated to my dear friends and colleagues
who are also my sisters in Christ:
Donna-Jean Breckenridge
Lynn Bruce
Wendi Capehart
Leslie Laurio
Anne White
Because in our work together over many years they have embodied
the vital harmony of truth, goodness, beauty, and love.

Contents

Foreword

Charlotte Mason lived about a century ago and wrote six volumes of her own plus much more in other publications. So when we find ourselves in the midst of her life's work, it should come as no surprise that people disagree about what it means to have a "Charlotte Mason education." Charlotte even left us twenty principles with which to navigate the deep waters of her thoughts. But how do we navigate the principles themselves? Are they all equal? Can we pop in anywhere amongst them and arrive at the same place? In her newest book, *In Vital Harmony*, Karen Glass offers us insight and guidance for this daunting task.

Choosing which principle we enter through first is vital. What if we declare the "habit of attention" the wicket gate of entry? We're apt to find ourselves herding small children into classrooms and teaching them to speak on command. We'll view Charlotte Mason through glasses tinted by habit training. This approach would look quite different than if we entered through, say, principle eighteen, "the way of reason."

Or maybe we find ourselves more in tune with "education is an atmosphere"—principle six—than with principle seven, "education is a discipline." This common misapplication of Charlotte Mason's ideas leads some educators to dismiss a Charlotte Mason education as something like unschooling. When "atmosphere" is the wicket gate, the result can be a continual lingering at the rose arbor with just a smidgen of Mozart thrown into the mix. Applying the twenty principles can get tricky, but we begin to see that it matters.

Thankfully, Karen Glass has done the scholarly work of studying Charlotte Mason's words thoroughly so as to understand how each of the twenty principles relates to the rest. Here in *In Vital Harmony* we find Karen helping us navigate that morass of ideas circulating as a Charlotte Mason education. *In Vital Harmony* pulls us out of our educational Slough of Despond and points us to the very wicket gate we need in order to arrive at the Celestial City of a true, good, beautiful, balanced, and contemporary Charlotte Mason education.

For many years Karen Glass has been quietly studying and sharing what she has learned about Charlotte Mason while homeschooling her own children and participating in the creation and upkeep of AmblesideOnline, a free Charlotte Mason curriculum. Karen has become the voice of reason untangling the many threads of narration, knowledge, and the twenty principles. In order to help us all come to a deeper understanding of what Charlotte Mason was saying, Karen has steadfastly kept her nose in Charlotte's books and the Armitt Museum and Library, which houses Charlotte's works.

After reading Karen's book *Consider This*, I knew Karen had a unique gift for analogy, logic, and a trustworthy way of seeing. Now in her latest book, she uses this gift to untangle much of the confusion we fall into when we shuffle the deck of the twenty principles haphazardly. I loved this book so much that I highlighted almost every page. Whether you're struggling to make sense of all the different aspects of a Charlotte Mason education or you've been a longtime friend of Charlotte Mason's works, *In Vital Harmony* is essential, and I'm so happy my friend Karen Glass wrote it.

—Cindy Rollins

Introduction

This book is a comprehensive look at the principles that make up the educational philosophy of Charlotte Mason. She was a British educator of the nineteenth and early twentieth centuries whose ideas have grown widespread in twenty-first-century America and are finding footholds in educational communities around the world. She presented a synopsis of her philosophy in the form of twenty principles that represent a complete body of thought. I am not going to alter them; however, I am going to present these principles in a different form. I want to express them and their relationships in contemporary language that will make them more comprehensible and relevant for today's parents and teachers. The simple list form in which Miss Mason presented them remains valid. I have included them in abbreviated form in this introduction, as well as in their original form in the appendix (page 171).

She was speaking to her country, her culture, and her time. We can still understand what she said, but it requires extra effort, similar to conversing with someone who speaks our language with an accent much different from our own. We use the same words, but subtle differences make communication a little harder. Everything from tempo to the emphasis on certain syllables to unfamiliar enunciation makes the effort to understand more difficult than it would be if we were speaking to someone who talks exactly like we do. So it is with Miss Mason.

She spoke to be understood—but she was speaking to the wordy Victorians and their successors, the Edwardians. She was speaking to British parents who lived over one hundred years ago and were so

1

familiar with the novels of the day that Miss Mason could name-drop a character from a book without mentioning the title or author and expect her readers to pick up the allusion. In a similar way, you would probably understand a reference to Indiana Jones or Darth Vader, but someone reading this book a hundred years in the future might not have any idea what those names mean. That's where most of us find ourselves when Miss Mason glibly refers to "'Joan and Peter' types of education" (a reference to a then-new novel by H.G. Wells) or "the immortal Mr. Chadband" (a minor character in Charles Dickens's *Bleak House*).

Miss Mason made certain assumptions about her readers and her culture that do not apply to twenty-first-century Americans. Does that make her principles unusable for us? Not at all—and that is the point where I'm going to begin. Principles do not change. A principle Plato observed and remarked upon was still true when Miss Mason established the Parents' National Educational Union (PNEU) over two thousand years later, and it is still true in the technology-swamped twenty-first century. Principles remain constant.

However, the way we talk about principles—and perhaps the aspects of them we choose to emphasize—might change. We may even say that it probably *should* change because our circumstances change. The essential principles of education are exactly as they have always been, but they remain living and do not become stale when they are turned around and examined afresh in light of current thought. One of Miss Mason's colleagues, Thomas Rooper, wrote:

> Sound principles that are old may easily be laid on the shelf and forgotten, unless in each successive generation a few industrious people can be found who will take the trouble to draw them forth from the storehouse. (*Educational Studies and Addresses*, p. 7)

Miss Mason did that very thing for her generation, but she reminded us as well that there is no last word to be said on education. We cannot limit our exploration of educational truths to the writings of other times and even less to the writings of a single author. Sound principles must be explored within the context of every age. During her lifetime, Miss Mason deliberately refrained from attaching her name to the principles she espoused because she knew it would strangle fresh insight. She wrote:

> We hold that education as a science must ever maintain a tentative attitude. The moment she frames a stereotyped creed represented by any given name or names of the past or present, she becomes formal and mechanical rather than spontaneous and living. The effort to define or limit in matters too broad and deep to be expressed in a definition or represented by a name is the history of all division whether in religion or education. (From a leaflet by Charlotte Mason, quoted in *The Story of Charlotte Mason* by Essex Cholmondeley, pp. 53–54)

While Miss Mason may not have presented every principle applicable to education, she did distill the essential elements that work together as a whole. For the sake of this work, I am going to assume her twenty principles represent a comprehensive and complete foundation upon which to build educational practices, which is why I include all twenty of them and add nothing to them. I have seen scores of children educated according to these principles from age six to graduation, and I am satisfied that nothing essential is missing.

A teacher who implements the principles set forth by Miss Mason has a complete set of ideas. One of the indications this is true is that they are generous and flexible enough to accommodate a variety of circumstances without being compromised. These principles work in classrooms, in homeschools, and with adults who are educating themselves.

Educational trends and fads tend to drive the practices of teachers and schools, making education seem like a frantic pursuit to keep up with something new. If we change our focus from what is *new* to what is universally *true*, we invite a more peaceful approach into our educational efforts. New ideas can be evaluated in light of the principles. If new ideas are sound, they will harmonize with the truths we understand. We have a firm foundation for education that will give us perspective about all the conflicting ideas in the air. We will be able to choose wisely and have confidence in what we are doing as teachers when we know we are standing upon solid educational truths.

Abbreviated Principles of Charlotte Mason

In addition to the full list of principles in the appendix, this shorter version is included here for reference as you read. I always refer to the principles by the numbers that Miss Mason gave them.

1. **Children are born** *persons.*
2. They are not born either good or bad, but with possibilities for good and for evil.
3. The principles of authority on the one hand, and of obedience on the other, are natural, necessary and fundamental.
4. These principles are limited by the respect due to the personality of children, which must not be encroached upon.
5. Therefore, we are limited to three educational instruments— the atmosphere of environment, the discipline of habit, and the presentation of living ideas.
6. When we say that *"education is an atmosphere,"* we do not mean that a child should be isolated in what may be called a "child-environment" but that we should take into account the educational value of his natural home atmosphere.
7. By *"education is a discipline,"* we mean the discipline of habits, formed definitely and thoughtfully, whether habits of mind or body.
8. In saying that *"education is a life,"* the need of intellectual and moral as well as of physical sustenance is implied. The mind feeds on ideas.
9. We hold that the child's mind is no mere sac to hold ideas; but is rather, if the figure may be allowed, a spiritual organism, with an appetite for all knowledge.
10. Such a doctrine as *e.g.* the Herbartian, that the mind is a receptacle, lays the stress of education (the preparation of knowledge in enticing morsels duly ordered) upon the teacher.

11. But we, believing that the normal child has powers of mind which fit him to deal with all knowledge proper to him, give him a full and generous curriculum.
12. *Education is the Science of Relations*; that is, that a child has natural relations with a vast number of things and thoughts.
13. In devising a SYLLABUS for a normal child, of whatever social class, three points must be considered: (a) He requires *much* knowledge. (b) The knowledge should be various. (c) Knowledge should be communicated in well-chosen language.
14. As knowledge is not assimilated until it is reproduced, children should "tell back" after a single reading or hearing: or should write on some part of what they have read.
15. A *single reading* is insisted on, because children have naturally great power of attention; but this force is dissipated by the re-reading of passages, and also, by questioning, summarising, and the like.
16. There are two guides to moral and intellectual self-management to offer to children, which we may call "the way of the will" and "the way of the reason."
17. *The way of the will*: Children should be taught to distinguish between "I want" and "I will."
18. *The way of reason*: We teach children not to "lean (too confidently) to their own understanding."
19. Children should be taught that the chief responsibility which rests on them *as persons* is the acceptance or rejection of ideas. To help them in this choice we give them principles of conduct, and a wide range of the knowledge fitted to them.
20. We allow no separation to grow up between the intellectual and "spiritual" life of children.

Part I

A Few Broad Essential Principles

A few broad essential principles cover the whole field.

—Charlotte Mason, *Home Education*

1

The Principle Thing

What if those two or three vitalizing educational principles could
be brought before parents?
—Charlotte Mason, from *The Story of Charlotte Mason*

Principles Govern Actions

Before I address Charlotte Mason's specific educational principles,
I want to address this question: "What is a principle?"
Miss Mason proposed:

> For what, after all, are principles but those motives of first impor-
> tance which govern us, move us in thought and action? (Charlotte
> Mason, *Philosophy of Education*, p. 62)

That is not a complete definition, but she hit upon a key point:
Principles should result in action. They are not something that
we simply declare with our mouths. We reveal our principles—the
motives that govern us—by our actions. The things we do, the choices
we make, the attitudes we display—all the behaviors and actions that
make up our lives—should be in harmony with the principles we
profess. It is in our actions that our principles manifest themselves.

Someone might say he believes in caring for the environment, but
does he recycle and conserve water or is he spraying pesticide on
his lawn? Our real principles, not just the ones we talk about, drive
our actions. There is a distinction between theory and practice: Does
a person's behavior match his professed principles? A person may

profess an idea quite vehemently, but if his actions do not match his words, that idea is not, in fact, his principle.

There are two kinds of principles, which we might call personal principles and universal principles. We can choose our own personal principles of life. We may decide to live as free spirits or according to rigid codes. A personal principle is simply a guiding idea, and it may be good or bad. We may make honesty our guiding principle, or we may think acquiring money is the greatest good in life. Whatever our principles may be, they will influence the decisions we make. Miss Mason explained that "our lives are ordered by our principles, good or bad" and lamented:

> There are always catch-words floating in the air, as, — "What's the good?" "It's all rot," and the like, which the vacant mind catches up for use as the basis of thought and conduct, as, in fact, paltry principles for the guidance of a life. (*Philosophy of Education*, p. 62)

Our personal principles govern our behavior. This is true whether they are good principles or bad ones. Nothing much has changed. The jaded young person who asserted in Miss Mason's day that "it's all rot" and declined to conform to conventions about education and employment looks very much like the young person today who declares "You only live once!" by way of a principle and barrels head-long into every thrill he can find.

In addition to the personal principles we choose to adhere to, there are universal principles—absolute principles—that operate in the world and cannot be circumvented. We must live by them or suffer the consequences. These principles can better be understood as laws— laws of nature—and Miss Mason did not hesitate to equate natural law with "Divine law" (Charlotte Mason, *Home Education*, p. 135).

Some Principles Are Laws

A principle that is a *law* is true and cannot be evaded. Miss Mason offered examples of laws like "fire burns" or "water flows" to illustrate the way our behavior is shaped by the laws we apprehend (*Home Education*, p. 10). For example, we know that water flows. If we want to put fresh flowers in a container, we pour water into something nonporous, such as glass or plastic, and not into a crocheted vase, however pretty it might be. We might put a quantity of potato chips into a too-small bowl, confidently heaping them above the edge, but we know it would be a mistake to try that with water.

In many towns water is stored in tanks high above the ground, so it will flow down to local homes. The ancient Romans built clever aqueducts that took advantage of the way water flows to bring it from great distances and deliver it where it was needed. On the same principle, we dig to find water that has flowed down, and sometimes we must dig deeply because water always flows down to the lowest level. We cannot choose whether or not water will flow in the same way that we choose our personal principles. We simply know it flows. We acknowledge this principle—this law of nature—and then we adapt our behavior in harmony with that knowledge and truth.

If we do not shape our behavior in accordance with the laws and principles of nature, we cannot escape the consequences. For example, there are laws of nature that govern healthy diet and exercise. We may choose to violate those laws, but we cannot escape the results of our choices, whatever they are. We can choose soda over water, sweets over vegetables, and highly processed foods over natural ingredients, but we cannot escape the laws that govern the health of the body. The natural consequences of violating those laws will surely follow.

Sometimes, we simply have no choice about following a law. For instance, we must live our lives in accordance with the law of gravity. We cannot choose to float or fly instead of walk across a room. If we were to leap from a high place, the law of gravity and not our own choice would determine our trajectory.

We are free to defy a principle—which is really an absolute truth, an immutable law—but we are not free to avoid the natural results. Airplanes do not fly by defying the laws of gravity and physics. Those laws govern every aspect of their design and manufacture. An engineer does not consult his personal taste or ask, "What's the hottest new trend in wing shape this year?" He asks, "What shape and curve and material will interact with the laws of physics to provide the best lift?" When we adhere very closely to the laws of nature and adapt to them well, many extraordinary things become possible.

There Are Natural Laws in Education

What does this have to do with education? Are there laws of nature—laws of mind—that correspond to natural laws such as the law of gravity or the law that fire burns? Miss Mason believed that there were such laws and that educational practices and behaviors should also be guided by those principles. In the same way that adhering strictly to the laws of physics enables a jet to soar through the air, adhering to the laws of education should yield stunning results. This becomes possible only by knowing what those laws are and then shaping our practices to harmonize with them.

Miss Mason wanted to offer the world a glimpse of the universal truths that govern the way the mind operates and learns, which would in turn govern the behavior of teachers and parents who are involved in the process of educating children. This is the whole premise of her educational philosophy—that there are principles and that knowing and following those principles gives us as parents and teachers the best chance of succeeding in our endeavors. We may walk with confidence, run with endurance, and perhaps even fly.

In the same way that we automatically shape our behavior around the principles we know—gravity pulls and fire burns—so understanding the educational principles will allow us to act intuitively in our knowledge of them. Miss Mason assured us:

> The parent who *sees his way*—that is, the exact force of method—to educate his child, will make use of every circumstance of the child's life almost without intention on his own part, so easy and spontaneous is a method of education based upon Natural Law. Does the child eat or drink, does he come, or go, or play—all the time he is being educated, though he is as little aware of it as he is of the act of breathing. (*Home Education*, p. 8)

This is the way that principles operate. When we deeply apprehend a principle, we act upon it instinctively. Without strenuous effort or tedious forethought, we behave in a way that harmonizes with that principle. You can build a fire in your fireplace without burning your house down or light a match in the woods for a campfire without starting a forest fire because you know how to live by the principle, which is a natural law, that fire burns.

Educational principles can operate in the same way. When we know them well, our educational choices and actions will be guided by our understanding. Knowing these principles does not mean simply being able to recite or identify them. We tell a toddler "the stove is hot," but that knowledge means little to him until he has touched it and felt the heat for himself. You may be aware of the educational principles Miss Mason has articulated for us at a superficial level without fully apprehending all that they mean. In order for them to guide your daily actions at an intuitive level, you must comprehend them as well as you comprehend that fire burns.

Charlotte Mason Identified Several Principles

There are twenty principles in Miss Mason's final book, *An Essay Towards a Philosophy of Education*. But are there actually twenty *primary* principles that you must know in order to implement her philosophy? Although today's educators often refer to her "twenty principles," she never talked about that number. Rather, she wrote:

> The fact is, that a few broad essential principles cover the whole field, and these once fully laid hold of, it is as easy and natural to act upon them as it is to act upon our knowledge of such facts as that fire burns and water flows. (*Home Education*, p. 10)

When I read that, I began to wonder: Which are those few essential principles—those two or three she wanted to bring before parents? Why shouldn't we make it clear to ourselves which principles are the primary ones? If we could grasp and understand the most important principles as well as we understand the fact that water flows, how much easier our educational efforts would be.

I began to examine Miss Mason's principles both individually and as a group. One of the principles is *education is the science of relations*, and I wanted to understand how the principles stood in relation to each other. Which ones were the most important—the *essential* ones?

As I pursued these questions and read through the Home Education series searching for these relationships, a picture emerged of a unity among the principles. Yes, there were a few that could be identified as primary. Miss Mason was clear about them. As I read and studied, it became evident to me that the two most essential principles are these: *Children are born persons* and *education is the science of relations.* These are the central principles, and all the rest of the principles fall into place around them, making a "coherent body of educational thought" (*Home Education*, preface).

After I had done my searching and thinking and had identified these two vital principles, I discovered that at the very beginning of her first book, Miss Mason had made this plain:

> The central thought, or rather body of thought, upon which I found, is the somewhat obvious fact that *the child is a person* with all the possibilities and powers included in personality. Some of the members which develop from this nucleus have been exploited from time to time by educational thinkers, and exist vaguely in the general common sense, a notion here, another there. One thesis, which is, perhaps, new, that *Education is the Science of Relations*, appears to me to solve the question of curricula, as showing that the object of education is to put a child in living touch with as much as may be of the life of Nature and of thought. Add to this one or two keys to self knowledge, and the educated youth goes forth with some idea of self management, with some pursuits, and many vital interests. (*Home Education*, Preface, emphasis added)

In this paragraph, she names those two principles that I had identified as the most vital, and she remarks, "Add to this one or two keys to self knowledge." These keys can also be found in the principles. Rather than exploring the principles in the list form in which they appear in Miss Mason's synopsis at the beginning of each of her books, the following chapters will unfold the principles as they relate to one another so that the "coherent body" of educational thought may be understood as a unified whole and not as a mere collection. Miss Mason assured us that what she offered was a "body of thought with various members working in vital harmony" (*Home Education*, preface). I hope to make both the various members and the vital harmony a little clearer for us all.

2

No Matter How Small

A person's a person, no matter how small.
—Dr. Seuss

Education Begins with a Basic Truth

Children are born persons. This is the first essential principle. It is also a universal truth, but like all truths it has more than one aspect and can be examined from many angles.

What does it mean that *children are born persons?* What does that imply? This bare statement demands an answer to the question "What is a person?" Until you know exactly what Charlotte Mason meant by it, the meaning of *children are born persons* is still obscure. It might have been somewhat unclear for her contemporaries, but it is even more so for our own. If you were to ask people to define what a person is, there is no guarantee you would get a consistent or even a coherent answer. Miss Mason took the time in her volumes to explain what she meant, and this principle—one of the essential, vital ones—deserves our thoughtful attention.

Nothing is of greater interest to people than themselves. This question—What is a person?—has engaged thinkers throughout the ages and continues to do so.

Is a person merely an embodied consciousness—a brain with arms and legs? We know people are conscious beings, and our self-awareness as humans is unique. We have language and reason. We create art and record our history. We play organized sports, construct governments, develop medicine, practice surgery, and build incredible

15

machines. We do things no other beings on earth do, and yet many of us suppose that our consciousness, self-awareness, and creativity are merely the result of our advanced physical brains. We wonder if similar consciousness could be created by technology. This speculation has been going on for a long time, and our view that artificial intelligence (AI) is possible, perhaps even inevitable, has affected our view of human intelligence. We have to some extent reached the point where we not only imagine computers as persons but also imagine persons as computers. Perhaps, we think, our minds are simply a network of neurons that rapidly *compute* or *process* the *data* that we encounter.

Both popular entertainment and science have caused the idea of viable AI to seep into the thinking of our culture. People are not certain about whether or not a computer could become a person or whether a person is like a computer. That uncertainty, which allows for the possibility that a person might be like a machine, has undermined the collective view of what it means to be a person. If we suspect that a machine could become a person, it is possible that a person is simply a biological machine. People discuss both sides of the question all the time, but as a culture we aren't sure.

Miss Mason did not share our uncertainty. She knew exactly what she meant by a *person*. While computers had not yet been invented during her lifetime, she understood what it meant to imagine that a person had no more than a material or biomechanical existence.

> The limitations of the real [as opposed to the ideal], with its one possible outcome, that man himself is a *congeries* [collection] of regulated atoms—that there is nothing in the universe but atoms and regulating laws—this doctrine is oppressive to the spirit of man. (Charlotte Mason, *Formation of Character*, p. 450)

Her use of the word *spirit* is our clue. When Miss Mason said that children are born persons, she was implying that the life of a person encompasses far more than mere physical presence. In order to understand this principle, we have to understand that personhood includes something more.

The most important part of a person—the thing that defines *personhood* or *self*—is not an amazing brain that processes millions of bits of data. The essence of a person is not confined to material existence. We may imagine that our consciousness has emerged as a result of the sheer volume of our processing ability, but that is not what makes a person. A person has a nonmaterial *mind* and a heart that *feels* and does not merely pump blood. The essence of the first principle is this: Children are born with active and able *minds*, not simply brains, and therefore education must address this nonmaterial, *spiritual* aspect of a person.

A Child Has a Mind

Miss Mason described an alternative view of psychical evolution that was proposed in her time: Just as a new baby has an undeveloped physical body that lacks the power of a grown person, so he also has an undeveloped mind and does not yet possess the intellect of a person.

> A baby is a huge oyster (says one eminent psychologist) whose business is to feed, and to sleep, and to grow. (Charlotte Mason, *Parents and Children*, p. 251)

Her contemporaries associated this process with evolution. They suggested that a child is not fully evolved at birth but needs to progress through several more stages before he is fully human and in possession of an intellect. Miss Mason explained their thinking:

> He is an evolutionist, and feels himself pledged to accommodate the child to the principles of evolution. Therefore the little person is supposed to go through a thousand stages of moral and intellectual development, leading him from the condition of the savage or ape to that of the intelligent and cultivated human being. (*Parents and Children*, p. 251)

She objected to this notion that the mind of a baby is no more than the mind of an oyster, and her objection has an educational application. If a baby has a mind that is undeveloped, not able to function at a high level, it would mean that knowledge must be dumbed down for him.

> The notion that an infant is a huge oyster, who by slow degrees, and more and more, develops into that splendid intellectual and

moral being, a full-grown man or woman, has been impressed
upon us so much of late years that we believe intellectual spoon-
meat to be the only food for what we are pleased to call "little
minds." (Charlotte Mason, *School Education*, p. 171)

Further, if a baby does not possess a mind of his own, the educator—whether parent or teacher—can shape it as he chooses, like
a lump of clay. If a baby has no mind of his own at birth, it must be
the role of the educator to develop one for him, and that is what some
people thought.

> But is the baby more than a "huge oyster"? That is the problem
> before us and hitherto educators have been inclined to answer
> in the negative. Their notion is that by means of a pull here, a
> push there, a compression elsewhere a person is at last turned out
> according to the pattern the educator has in mind. (*Philosophy of
> Education*, pp. 33–34)

Miss Mason dismissed this inadequate view of children, and she
considered the children themselves to be the ones who disproved the
theory. She laid out the intellectual achievements of children—for
example, mastery of a language and sometimes more than one—
during the first two years of life. She offered evidence of imagination
and reason in these little ones that any parent could verify.

> As soon as he can speak, he lets us know that he has pondered the
> "cause why" of things and perplexes us with a thousand questions.
> His "why?" is ceaseless. (*Philosophy of Education*, p. 37)

Because babies were viewed in a way that disregarded their intelligence, Miss Mason began her list of principles with her alternative point of view based on universal truth. It is nothing less than a
philosophical statement about the nature of mankind with a specific
application to very young persons. Our view of personhood makes a
very great difference in the educational practices used, even in the
earliest years. Are we dealing with a child who has an alert, intelligent mind or a witless oyster? She had no doubts, and she assured us
that:

> If we have not proved that a child is born a person with a mind
> as complete and as beautiful as his beautiful little body, we can

at least show that he always has all the mind he requires for his occasions; that is, that his mind is the instrument of his education and that *his education does not produce his mind.* (*Philosophy of Education*, p. 36)

Miss Mason used certain vocabulary very consistently, and we will understand her better if we pay attention to it. She used the word *brain* when she referred to that physical organ, but when she used the word *mind*, she was always referring to this spiritual, nonmaterial aspect of a person. It provides the foundation for the way we must educate.

> I have avoided philosophical terms, using only names in common use,—body and soul, body and mind, body, soul and spirit,— because these represent ideas that we cannot elude and that convey certain definite notions; and these ideas must needs form the basis of our educational thought.
>
> We must know something about the material we are to work upon if the education we offer is not to be scrappy and superficial. (*Philosophy of Education*, p. 65)

Because she rejected the notion that babies were intellectually deficient in any way, the first principle includes the word *born*—"Children are *born* persons"—rather than merely "Children are persons." She underscored the fact that the *mind* of a person—a lively intelligence that is self-existing within each of us—is present from the very beginning. Education does not produce mind. Today, the concept of mind itself might be the more vital aspect of this principle to emphasize—children are born persons, yes, but we are all persons with *minds.* We are not machines or computers processing data.

Our Culture Needs to Understand the Idea of Mind

Today we need to address the nonmaterial nature of a person. A mind is not a brain. Historically, we have used different words to refer this aspect of a person—spirit, soul, mind, intellect, even heart. But the salient point is this: It is not physical. It is not made up of moving parts or neurons or even atoms. It cannot be observed by any physical mode of detection we possess. Every time you say "I," you underscore your individual existence as a separate person who possesses what we can only call *personality*. You are you, and you can think and feel and reason and communicate in a way that is both unique to you and common with all other persons.

We are unique persons. We are not interchangeable, like so many identical parts manufactured according to a set of blueprints. Men and women go home to their own spouses, not any random person. Children are raised by their own parents, not whichever adults happen to be nearby. We cherish special friends, and an incidental stranger sitting at the next table will not fill that role. If one of us is lost, we are lost from the earth forever. Everyone who has suffered the death of someone close to them knows this. A person cannot be replaced.

At the same time, however, every person walking on the planet shares our *personhood*, creating a universal brotherhood among mankind to which we give lip service even when we do not act and live by that principle. We have learned, when we are being absolutely honest, to look at a person of a different race, gender, belief, or culture and to acknowledge that "He is like me." We are the same because we share the same feelings and desires. We want the same fundamental things—safety, happiness, love—even when we have conflicting ideas about how to achieve those things.

Miss Mason was able to take for granted that her readers understood this nonmaterial aspect of being a person. As you read through her writings, you can observe her distinct use of *mind* rather than *brain* when she referred to this nonphysical intellect or soul that a person possesses. She believed education should be directed toward this nonmaterial part of a person. The physical brain has its role to play, but it is the mind that is the person. The distinction is clear:

> I am anxious to bring before teachers the fact that a child comes
> into their hands with a mind of amazing potentialities: he has a
> brain too, no doubt, the organ and instrument of that same mind,
> as a piano is not music but the instrument of music. (*Philosophy
> of Education*, p. 38)

Miss Mason wrote, "We believe the thinking, invisible soul and acting, visible body to be one" (*School Education*, p. 63). A person has both a physical body and a spiritual mind, and that is the essence of the principle that *children are born persons*.

True Education Requires a Right Understanding of Mind

Today we sometimes look at computers and imagine we are getting closer and closer to the emergence of genuine AI—a machine that would be a person. But a person is not a machine, and we must not let our fascination with technology undermine our view of personhood. The children we are teaching are so much more, and if we do not recognize all that they are, we can only fall short in our efforts to teach them. Miss Mason worried that educators in her time would undervalue children's intelligence.

> As a matter of fact, we do not *realise* children, we under-estimate them; in the divine words, we "despise" them, with the best intentions in the world, because we confound the immaturity of their frames, and their absolute ignorance as to the relations of things, with spiritual impotence: whereas the fact probably is, that never is intellectual power so keen, the moral sense so strong, spiritual perception so piercing, as in those days of childhood which we regard with a supercilious, if kindly, smile. (*Parents and Children*, p. 260)

We are also at risk. If we do not appreciate what it means that a child is a person with both a brain and a mind, our educational efforts will go astray. Our data-processing view of persons may lead us to suppose children can be taught the way computers are programmed—that certain commands and processes will produce predictable results. Remember that our principles—those ideas we understand or believe to be true—will determine our behavior. If a teacher believes that a person possesses only a material brain that responds to stimuli, the educational practices that grow out of that belief will resemble teaching rats to run through a maze. Any method that fails to address children as they actually are will fail to educate them.

We must ground ourselves with educational principles—universal laws that will govern what we do. In Miss Mason's educational paradigm, we begin by understanding that a person has a spirit—that children are not merely physical beings with a clever brain to record and process data. We are educating *persons* who have *minds*. Merely acknowledging this (without supposing we fully comprehend all that it means) is a step toward wisdom because it embraces reality.

It is in many ways a matter of faith or belief. There is no way to prove with scientific evidence that a person has a spirit, a nonphysical existence. It is also not possible to disprove that a person has a spirit. Whether you believe in mind or do not believe in mind, it is a matter of belief and not subject to the laws of physical evidence. We cannot see love, respect, consideration, or sympathy. Do those things not exist because we cannot prove their existence with a scientific experiment? Of course not. So it is with mind—we take it on trust, and truly our personal experience supports our faith. We believe in mind as we believe in love—because we have experienced it.

And when we believe in mind—when we embrace the principle that *children are born persons* with lively minds—our educational efforts will be set on the right path. Miss Mason wrote:

> We have ceased to believe in mind...and we have come to believe that children are inaccessible to ideas or any knowledge.
>
> The message for our age is, *Believe in mind, and let education go straight as a bolt to the mind of the pupil.* (Philosophy of Education, pp. 259–60, emphasis added)

Having established the principle that *children are born persons*, several adjunct principles emerge, which we will discuss later. For now, it is important to appreciate that this first principle gives us a certain view of personhood that is one of the essential principles that must govern everything we do. As we approach the topic of education, it is very tempting to skip this part of the process—thinking through the principles at work—but the risk is too great. We cannot develop the best and most effective methods of teaching until we understand exactly what kind of person we are teaching. We are educating a mind—a soul—not a brain.

3

The Captain Idea

The method of study is to be specially directed to demonstrating
as it were the "reign of law"—the general connection and affinity
of these subject-matters with one another—and to test in the
student the power of grasping such a connection.
—Bernard Bosanquet

Personal Relations

Science and Relations

The next principle that is one of the two most vital is the twelfth
principle: *Education is the science of relations.* Charlotte Mason called
this the guiding principle of education:

> We do not sufficiently realise the need for unity of principle in
> education. We have no Captain Idea which shall marshal for us
> the fighting host of educational ideas which throng the air; so, in
> default of a guiding principle, a leading idea, we feel ourselves at
> liberty to pick and choose...Everyone feels himself at liberty to
> do that which is right in his own eyes with regard to the educa-
> tion of his children.
>
> Let it be our negative purpose to discourage in every way we
> can the educational faddist, that is, the person who accepts a one-
> sided notion in place of a universal idea as his educational guide.
> Our positive purpose is to present, in season and out of season,
> one such universal idea; that is, that education is the science of
> relations. (*School Education*, pp. 160–161)

Education is the science of relations is the captain idea that is going to direct all our educational endeavors. However, it will not take its role as *your* captain until you make this principle your own. In order to do that fully, you must spend some time exploring both the breadth and depth of this universal idea.

My own feeling about the word *science* in this statement is that Miss Mason was using it because it was a popular idea, a buzzword that caught the attention of her contemporaries. For them, science was the most exciting thing happening in the world. New discoveries were changing life as it had been for centuries before their very eyes. It was the industrial age. Communication and travel were revolutionized. She hinted at this wonder and change by marveling at the telegraph.

> In those remote pre-war days we were enormously startled by the discovery of wireless telegraphy. That communications should pass through almost infinite space without sign or sound or obvious channel and arrive instantly at their destination took away our breath. We had the grace to value the discovery for something more than its utility; we were awed in the presence of a law which had always been there but was only now perceived. (*Philosophy of Education*, p. 68)

In Britain as well as in America, people used the word *science* for everything—for example, they began to modernize housekeeping by calling it "household science." There is probably no point in trying to be precise about what Miss Mason meant by the word *science* in her principle because she never defined it herself. It is sufficient to understand that science in the Victorian era was simply something exciting to be explored, and she shared the common fascination with it. She had a reverence for science as knowledge from God, calling it a "mode of revelation." A working definition for science as the term was commonly used might be "an exploration of knowledge," and the primary topic of exploration in this case is *relations*. *Education is the science of relations* means that relations are the primary concern of education, and we must explore all that this means.

The Law of Relations

This is not merely a good idea that can be accepted or discarded at will. Miss Mason reminded us that we are dealing with principles— natural laws of the universe:

> We labour under the mistake of supposing that there is no natural law or inherent principle according to which a child's course of studies should be regulated. (*Philosophy of Education*, p. 156)

On the contrary, there is a principle at work, and just as we had to understand what Miss Mason meant by *person* in the first principle, we must understand all that she means by *relations* in this principle. Her appreciation for science yields a clue:

> But for the most part science as she is taught leaves us cold; the utility of scientific discoveries does not appeal to the best that is in us, though it makes a pretty urgent and general appeal to our lower avidities. But the fault is not in science—that mode of revelation which is granted to our generation, may we reverently say?—but in our presentation of it by means of facts and figures and demonstrations that mean no more to the general audience than the point demonstrated, never showing the wonder and magnificent reach of the law unfolded. (*Philosophy of Education*, p. 318)

There is a way of teaching that "leaves us cold." That would be the opposite of forming a relation. Knowledge can be utilitarian—useful— without creating any interest, wonder, or delight. Miss Mason made our guiding principle plain: "Education should aim at giving knowledge '*touched with emotion*'" (*School Education*, p. 220).

Rather than leaving us cold, education should produce the warmth of interest and pleasure in the knowledge we meet. This principle tells us that our primary task as educators is to help a child establish these warm relations with all kinds of knowledge.

> Education is the Science of Relations; that is, that a child has natural relations with a vast number of things and thoughts: so we must train him upon physical exercises, nature, handicrafts, science and art, and upon *many living books*; for we know that our

business is, not to teach him all about anything, but to help him make valid, as many as may be of

"Those first born affinities, That fit our new existence to existing things." (*Philosophy of Education*, p. xxx)

With all the realms of knowledge before us and the need to establish relations everywhere, the task can seem overwhelming. Nevertheless, we cannot arbitrarily decide to deprive a child of knowledge that he naturally wants to know. While this principle encompasses much, it begins with the simple, natural introduction of a child to all the things that will interest him if he gets a chance to meet them.

Types of Relations

To make the great task of developing relations with what we must learn more manageable, Miss Mason divided knowledge into three categories—knowledge of God, knowledge of man, and knowledge of the universe. All the things a person wants to know lie within these three categories. Because a person is a spiritual being, he needs a relationship with the Spirit who is also the Creator—this forms the most vital aspect of education. In the realm of *knowledge of man,* we find history, art, literature, and language as well as architecture, music, and poetry—all the ways man expresses himself and communicates with others. *Knowledge of the universe* includes firsthand exposure to nature—whatever of nature is available—forests, water, desert sand, or rocky mountains. It includes the opportunity to explore physical possibilities such as climbing and swimming and rowing, as well as fine-motor skills such as clay modeling or woodworking. Children should have a chance to handle things for themselves and develop an understanding—a relationship—with everything that is available, including the knowledge found in books.

This is the beginning of the science of relationships, but relationships go much further, and Miss Mason knew that the personal relationships a child forms with knowledge must expand to include the recognition of the relationships that exist in the universe.

Universal Relations

The Breadth of Relations

We may develop relationships for ourselves, and it is very pleasant to do so, but there are also relationships already in place. Nothing is completely isolated. All the various kinds of knowledge are bound together whether we perceive it or not, but it is our delight to discover the connections. John Muir wrote, "When we try to pick out anything by itself, we find it hitched to everything else in the universe" (*My First Summer in the Sierra*, p. 157).

Miss Mason understood the same thing. All knowledge is connected, and she considered it nothing less than wisdom to recognize those relations in all their aspects.

> Now what is wisdom, philosophy? Is it not the recognition of *relations*? First, we have to understand relations of time and space and matter, the natural philosophy which made up so much of the wisdom of Solomon; then, by slow degrees, and more and more, we learn that moral philosophy which determines our relations of love and justice and duty to each other: later, perhaps, we investigate the profound and puzzling subject of the inter-relations of our own most composite being, mental philosophy. And in all these and beyond all these we apprehend, slowly and feebly, the highest relation of all, the relation to God, which we call religion. *In this science of the relations of things consists what we call wisdom.* (*Parents and Children*, pp. 258–59, emphasis added)

The first step in forming relations is to become personally acquainted with something concrete—maple trees or tulips or George Washington or a painting by Leonardo DaVinci. Next, we begin to appreciate more abstract relations about ourselves and our place in the brotherhood of mankind, as well as our relations to God. But these things do not exist separately, as if each were in a different box. Our understanding should expand so that we perceive that *all* knowledge is connected. Miss Mason wanted us to apprehend that all knowledge is joined by a unity of "the relations which bind all things to all other things" (*Parents and Children*, p. 259).

In the same way that we acknowledge the law of gravity, this vision of the unity of knowledge is a universal principle—a law of the very nature of the universe—that we must acknowledge in order to achieve all that is possible with education. This relational way of understanding knowledge is a *synthetic* understanding. We are not tearing things apart and destroying connections; we are learning how they fit together and recognizing their wholeness and unity.

Another way of speaking about this relational approach to knowledge is to call it a *poetic* understanding of the world. In his book *Poetic Knowledge*, Dr. James Taylor describes this kind of knowledge as an act of knowing that involves both external and internal senses. You experience something with your sense of sight or touch or hearing, but you also have an internal reaction to it—your feelings about what you've encountered. These two aspects of knowing, occurring together, are natural—just as Miss Mason told us. We naturally have a desire to form relations with all kinds of knowledge. She said of the child:

> We endeavour that he shall have relations of pleasure and intimacy established with as many as possible of the interests proper to him; not learning a slight or incomplete smattering about this or that subject, but plunging into vital knowledge, with a great field before him which in all his life he will not be able to explore. In this conception we get that "touch of emotion" which vivifies knowledge, for it is probable that we *feel* only as we are brought into our proper vital relations. (*School Education*, p. 223)

Synthetic, poetic, relational knowledge encompasses both the information involved and the intimacy of the learner with that knowledge. Education is not simply a matter of acquiring information but of encountering knowledge and allowing it to change us. As we learn to care about various things—things of the natural world or personal virtues such as honesty—our feelings will motivate us to act because of what we know. In this way, knowledge becomes virtue in a person's life.

The Depth of Relations

The opposite of this warm, relational approach to knowledge, which fosters emotions, is analysis. Analysis encourages us to break things down, and while there is a role for it with mature thinkers, it does not foster relationships. Miss Mason wrote:

> We have analysed until the mind turns in weariness from the broken fragments. (*Philosophy of Education*, p. 166)

Because we are persons, our hearts desire wholeness and intimacy and relationship. Sterilized, unconnected fragments of information have no appeal for us. Because they do not inspire us to care, they do not motivate us to act.

Poetic, relational knowledge is possible for a person only because a person has a spiritual nature, as we saw with the first principle. It is more than data. It is why a computer is not a person. A person can understand why "A tree that looks at God all day, / And lifts her leafy arms to pray" (from "Trees" by Joyce Kilmer) is more than mere information; it is also a beautiful thought, beautifully expressed. A person can understand that William Wordsworth was writing poetry when he wrote this stanza from "I Wandered Lonely as a Cloud":

> I saw a crowd
> A host, of golden daffodils;
> Beside the lake, beneath the trees,
> Fluttering and dancing in the breeze.

The sentence "I saw some daffodils by the lake" is merely a statement of fact, and as persons we feel the difference. This poetic understanding of the universe is rooted in love—in caring. If we go back to our understanding of the difference between a brain and a mind, a brain can only know a fact, but a cultivated mind can appreciate it and reflect upon its meaning in a larger context. Miss Mason told us:

> There is no doubt that this fact-lore is an invaluable possession. But it is not culture; it does not, necessarily, produce a cultivated mind, the habits of reading and reflection:—

> "A primrose by the river's brim
> A yellow primrose is to him,
> And it is nothing more" — (*Formation of Character*, p. 184)

This poetic, relational kind of knowledge is possible only to persons who possess a heart and a mind. These relationships are not only possible; they are the birthright of a person. Emotionally, a child who does not have the chance to experience love and relationships in a family is deprived of important bonds. The same is true in the intellectual realm of education. The child who never has the opportunity to develop relationships with art, music, nature, literature, history, and much more may feel the lack all his life. As teachers, we want children to find joy in learning.

> Thou hast set my feet in a large room; should be the glad cry of every intelligent soul. Life should be all *living*, and not merely a tedious passing of time; not all doing or all feeling or all thinking—the strain would be too great—but, all living; that is to say, we should be in touch wherever we go, whatever we hear, whatever we see, with some manner of vital interest. We cannot *give* the children these interests; we prefer that they should never say they have learned botany or conchology, geology or astronomy. The question is not,—how much does the youth *know*? when he has finished his education—but how much does he *care*? and about how many orders of things does he care? In fact, how large is the room in which he finds his feet set? and, therefore, how full is the life he has before him? (*School Education*, pp. 170–71)

This often-quoted paragraph from *School Education* gives us a glimpse of the science of relations. It reminds us that forming relationships—learning to care about many things—is the object of education. Also, the words "Thou hast set my feet in a large room" remind us that there is a unity to all knowledge. Knowledge is not pictured as a house with different rooms, separated by walls and isolated by doors. We have *one* room—a room that is enlarged by every relationship with knowledge that we form.

Only a person can love knowledge and learn to care about many things. That is the crux of the matter, and that is why *children are born persons* and *education is the science of relations* are the two central principles in Miss Mason's educational philosophy. These are the ones that bind all the rest together. These are the two principles that we must comprehend first. If you take the time to make sure you understand all that is meant in these two principles, you have the vital essence of her philosophy. These two principles are like two torches, creating two large pools of light that illuminate all that can be done in education.

Principle Relations

The Principles Are Related to Each Other

Once we understand that these two principles—*children are born persons* and *education is the science of relations*—form the core of Miss Mason's philosophy, we can begin to examine the rest of the principles within their framework. All the rest of the principles can be related to one or both of these two.

The twentieth principle is:

> We allow no separation to grow up between the intellectual and "spiritual" life of children, but teach them that the Divine Spirit has constant access to their spirits, and is their continual Helper in all the interests, duties, and joys of life. (*Philosophy of Education*, p. xxxi)

Because this principle mentioned the Divine Spirit, I originally supposed it must be one of the few essential principles. However, as I explored the relationships of the principles, I came to realize that such a way of thinking was actually *violating* the principle. If I imagined that *this* principle was spiritual and the other principles were *less* spiritual, I was in fact allowing a separation in my mind between things intellectual and things spiritual. I had to correct my thinking, and when I did, I realized that all the principles belong to one category—nothing intellectually true can be unspiritual. Miss Mason believed in the sacredness as well as the unity of all knowledge:

> All knowledge, dealt out to us in such portions as we are ready for, is sacred; knowledge is, perhaps, a beautiful whole, a great unity, embracing God and man and the universe, but having many parts which are not comparable with one another in the sense of less or more, because all are necessary and each has its functions. (*Philosophy of Education*, p. 324)

When I stopped assuming its overtly spiritual language made it more important than the other principles, I was able to see that this principle is an aspect of the vital principle that _education is the science of relations_. Wisdom is the science of relations, we are told, and the Holy Spirit is the source of every kind of knowledge we can encounter—of poetry and music and art—but also the source of mundane knowledge such as when to sow seed and how to prepare bread. Miss Mason often referred to a passage in Isaiah which illustrates that God is the source of even what we think of as common knowledge:

> Doth the plowman plow all day to sow? doth he open and break the clods of his ground? When he hath made plain the face thereof, doth he not cast abroad the fitches and scatter the cummin, and cast in the principal wheat and the appointed barley and the rye in their place? For his God doth instruct him to discretion, and doth teach him. (Isaiah 28:24–26, KJV)

There is nothing we can know about language or literature or art or music or physics or chemistry or engineering that does not have its source in God's own law and truth for the universe. All knowledge is connected because it springs from a single source, and that source is God.

> This idea of all education springing from and resting upon our relation to Almighty God is one which we have ever laboured to enforce. We take a very distinct stand upon this point. We do not merely give a _religious_ education, because that would seem to imply the possibility of some other education, a secular education, for example. But we hold that all education is divine, that every good gift of knowledge and insight comes from above, that the Lord the Holy Spirit is the supreme educator of mankind, and that the culmination of all education (which may, at the same time, be reached by a little child) is that personal knowledge of and intimacy with God in which our being finds its fullest perfection. (_School Education_, p. 95)

Miss Mason referred to this as the "Great Recognition" that educators are called upon to make—that all knowledge is unified and arises from a common source. This is the ultimate relationship that "binds all things to all other things." Because all knowledge comes from God, we cannot say that some things we learn are sacred and other things are secular, or apart from God. We must be careful not to allow those distinctions to be made.

We Must Avoid Hindering Relations

Brought down to a practical level, I think the twentieth principle, as Miss Mason has given it to us, is an outworking of what she called the *code of the education* in the Gospels:

> It is summed up in three commandments, and all three have a negative character, as if the chief thing required of grown-up people is that they should do no sort of injury to the children: *Take heed that ye* OFFEND *not—*DESPISE *not—*HINDER *not—one of these little ones.* (Home Education, p. 12)

The negative character of those statements is echoed by this principle that urges us to *allow no separation*. If education is the science of relations, and if all things are bound to all other things, then we should not hinder a child's thinking by allowing an element of separation to be introduced into his education. We must not allow a child to believe that intellectual pursuits are one thing and spiritual pursuits are of another kind altogether. That was the error I initially made while thinking about this principle, and it is an easy error to fall into.

Miss Mason told us explicitly that there are *not* two kinds of education—religious and secular. This is a vitally key point. When we ponder all that is meant by *education is the science of relations*, we must remember that our relations are not in this life and in this world only. There are eternal relations—spiritual relations—and education that is fulfilling all that education should do will never examine intellectual pursuits as if they were in some way disconnected from spiritual truths. In order to remain whole as persons, we must appreciate the wholeness of knowledge.

> Our nature craves after unity. The travail of thought, which is going on to-day and has gone on as long as we have any record of men's thoughts, has been with a view to establishing some principle for the unification of life. Here we have the scheme of a magnificent unity. We are apt to think that piety is one thing, that

> our intellectual and artistic yearnings are quite another matter, and that our moral virtues are pretty much matters of inheritance and environment, and have not much to do with our conscious religion. Hence, there come discords into our lives, discords especially trying to young and ardent souls who want to be good and religious, but who cannot escape from the overpowering drawings of art and intellect and mere physical enjoyment; they have been taught to consider that these things are, for the most part, alien to the religious life, and that they must choose one or the other; they do choose, and the choice does not always fall upon those things which, in our unscriptural and unphilosophical narrowness, we call the things of God. (*School Education*, pp. 154–55)

Miss Mason included this warning in her principles because of the harm that arises if a child begins to think that the knowledge that is so interesting and compelling for him is something apart from God, rather than a gift from Him.

> In fact our attitude with regard to our own intellectual processes leads to that disturbing sense of duality which causes the shipwreck of many lives, the distressing unrest of others, and the easy drifting of many more. Our thinking is not a separate thing from our conduct and our prayers, or even from our bodily well-being. Man is not several entities. He is one spirit (visibly expressed in bodily form), with many powers. He can work and love and pray and live righteously, but all these are the outcome of the manner of thoughts he thinks. (*School Education*, p. 114)

"The manner of thoughts he thinks" is the conception he holds of the world, the principles and beliefs that he begins to apprehend for himself. If he begins to think that God is not interested in small things as well as great, discord disturbs the unity and relationship that should form our educational pursuits.

All Relations Are Related to God

The Bible reminds us that a God who is infinitely big is also infinitely small. There is nothing beneath his notice and care. He sees a mere sparrow that falls, and He adorns the lowly grasses of the field with beauty that is divine in nature. If this is true, we can conceive that the way an Archimedes screw works, for example, or a pulley, is a thing that began as an idea in the mind of God and was realized in the world because that idea was perceived by the mind of person.

So it may be with everything in the world—all the things that interest us: a story, a poem, a painting, a concerto, but also a piece of jewelry or a refrigerator or a chair. These things begin as ideas, and ideas live and grow as they are passed from mind to mind. Because we are spiritual persons, we can discern ideas and form relationships with almost anything at all.

> Once begotten, the idea seems to survive indefinitely. It is painted in a picture, written in a book, carved into a chair, or only spoken to someone who speaks it again, who speaks it again, who speaks it again, so that it goes on being spoken, for how long? Who knows! (*School Education*, pp. 69–70)

Miss Mason quoted Coleridge's assertion that God even prepares certain minds to receive great new ideas that perhaps the world had not perceived before, citing Columbus as an example. He had an idea— an idea whose source must be God—and discovered a new world. She marveled at the telegraph and saw the principles behind it as nothing less than a newly revealed truth that God had allowed the world to perceive.

> Our piety, our virtue, our intellectual activities, and, let us add, our physical perfections, are all fed from the same source, God Himself; are all inspired by the same Spirit, the Spirit of God. The ages which held this creed were ages of mighty production in every kind; the princely commerce of Venice was dignified and sobered by this thought of the divine inspiration of ideas—ideas of trade, ideas of justice and fair balance and of utility. (*School Education*, p. 155)

If this is true, we must believe that the technology we enjoy today is also the result of ideas that God has allowed the world to comprehend. We must understand that we are persons with spiritual minds, and the Spirit of the universe is the source of everything we can know, whether it be mathematical relationships or the way electrons flow that allows for the creation of a silicon chip. We must perceive that everything we detect with our senses is the result of an idea that has been given form. Even if we comprehend these truths only partially, the result is a sound foundation for our thinking in an integrated, healthy way. We don't have to fear the rupture of separation that classifies knowledge as either sacred or secular. All the things we learn—grammar, geography, the habits of the insects in our backyard—put us in touch with God. Miss Mason assured us:

> But once the intimate relation, the relation of Teacher and taught in all things of the mind and spirit, be fully recognised, our feet are set in a large room; there is space for free development in all directions, and this free and joyous development, whether of intellect or heart, is recognised as a Godward movement. (*Parents and Children*, p. 275)

Relations Provide Unity and Harmony

By understanding the twentieth principle (allow no separation) as an aspect of the twelfth principle—*education is the science of relations*—we have a clearer understanding of just how vital and far-reaching this principle is. Notice that Miss Mason used the analogy of a large room to remind us of both our personal relations to knowledge and our relation to the Giver of knowledge. It is another strong hint that the twentieth principle is part of the *science of relations*. This principle encompasses all knowledge as a unified whole that cannot exist apart from God because He is the source of all knowledge. The result of this recognition, when no separation divides sacred knowledge from secular, is a holy joy and wonder in learning.

> A small English boy of nine living in Japan, remarked, "Isn't it fun, Mother, learning all these things? Everything seems to fit into something else." (*Philosophy of Education*, pp. 156–57)

When paired with the first principle—*children are born persons*—we can fully appreciate what the twentieth principle is trying to say—allow no separation here. These are educational principles, but they cannot be removed from the greater truths of which they are a part.

Rather than thinking of the twentieth principle as religious or theological (as we are wont to do because it mentions the Holy Spirit), consider the role of the Holy Spirit as the educator of mankind. Because the Spirit is the source of all kinds of knowledge, no pursuit of knowledge—even electronics or car repair or cooking—is wholly apart from Him. This particular relationship is possible because we are persons, and we have both a spiritual aspect that is reached by ideas and a physical aspect that works and acts and creates in the world.

> Such a recognition of the work of the Holy Spirit as the Educator of mankind, in things intellectual as well as in things moral and spiritual, gives us "new thoughts of God, new hopes of Heaven," a sense of harmony in our efforts and of acceptance of all that we are. (*Parents and Children*, p. 276)

In her writing, Miss Mason returned to these two vital principles again and again—*children are born persons* with a spiritual mind, and the function of a person is to form and understand relationships. The twentieth principle is corollary to the primary principle that *education is the science of relations*. As we shall see, all the rest of the principles are also related to one or both of these two primary principles. They form the core of Miss Mason's philosophy of education, a unity of various parts operating in vital harmony.

4

Finely Wrought Metal

Character is as finely wrought metal beaten into shape and beauty.
—Charlotte Mason, *A Philosophy of Education*

The Second Educational Principle Highlights the Task of Education

Once *children are born persons* is understood to be a central, primary principle, it is easy to discover that the principles which follow it are aspects of that basic idea. You could add the words "because children are born persons" to the beginning of the next several principles. The second principle says:

> They are not born either good or bad, but with possibilities for good and for evil. (*Philosophy of Education*, p. xxiv)

In order to understand the implications of this principle, we can consider the opposite, positive statement: Children are born either good or bad. This presents several possibilities: Perhaps some children are born good and some children are born bad. Maybe all children are born good, or all children are born bad. Which of these ideas was Charlotte Mason refuting when she asserted "they are not born either good or bad"? The answer seems to be that she was refuting all of them, not for the sake of argument but to bring to the fore the primary object of education.

It is tempting to interpret this principle theologically and assume she was talking about sin and guilt and eternal things, but these are educational principles. Miss Mason wanted us to think about the principles (which are *laws*) that govern education and what education is for. Saving a sinful soul is not one of the things that education may achieve. She made it clear that the remedy for sin is a Savior:

> Here is a thought to be brought tenderly before the child in the moments of misery that follow wrong-doing. "My poor little boy, you have been very naughty to-day! Could you not help it?" "No, mother," with sobs. "No, I suppose not; but there is a way of help." And then the mother tells her child how the Lord Jesus is our Saviour, because He saves us *from our sins*. (*Home Education*, p. 351)

Character, on the other hand, is something we ourselves must undertake to nurture in our children. Education cannot save us from sin, but it *can* influence character, and Miss Mason believed that "to direct and assist the evolution of character is the chief office of education" (*Parents and Children*, p. 233).

If the primary objective of education is to develop character, we ought to be able to find that idea in the principles, and that is what we do find here. The point Miss Mason was making is that a child's character is not established—predetermined—at birth. Children do not have a good *character* when they are born, nor do they have an evil character. They have no character as yet. They have possibilities and tendencies—predispositions to certain traits that may be good or bad. But what will they become?

The work of education is to support and direct the good tendencies while discouraging and uprooting, as far as possible, the bad ones. The result will be character (as we will see later, this is closely tied to the idea that a person has a will), and this educational task does not dispense with our need for a Savior. This principle reminds us that we have a responsibility to help our children develop a virtuous character in order to serve a Savior well. We all know believing people whose lives do not match their beliefs, and that is what Miss Mason hoped education could help correct.

We Must Believe We Can Influence Character

If a parent cannot influence the character of a child—if a person cannot improve his own character by making better choices—then there is nothing for education to do. The "nature vs. nurture" discussion is still going on today. Some believe it is nature—birth and genetic inheritance—that has the primary influence on who we are. Others think that nurture—the external influences that guide us as we learn and grow—has the greater impact. Miss Mason did not deny the power of our natural tendencies but urged us to remember that they should not be left unchecked.

> We are not meant to grow up in a state of nature. There is something simple, conclusive, even idyllic, in the statement that So-and-so is "natural." What more would you have?...."It's human nature," we say, when stormy Harry snatches his drum from Jack; when baby Marjorie, who is not two, screams for Susie's doll. So it is, and for that very reason it must be dealt with early. Even Marjorie must be taught better. "I always finish teaching my children obedience before they are one year old," said a wise mother [Susannah Wesley]; and any who know the nature of children, and the possibilities open to the educator, will say, Why not? Obedience in the first year, and all the virtues of the good life as the years go on; every year with its own definite work to show in the training of character. (*Parents and Children*, p. 65)

There is no settled answer to the "nature vs. nurture" question. We can find half a dozen books and articles on the subject written within the last five years—possibly within the last five months. Educators today are still talking about this. Miss Mason believed entirely that it was the duty of the educator—particularly the parents—to teach children virtue in the form of character. Nature alone is not enough.

Miss Mason reminded us, "Nature, left to herself, produces a waste" (*Formation of Character*, p. 24). Children are not "born good"—the doctrine of Rousseau and Locke—only to be corrupted by external influences, so that a parent's primary responsibility would be only to avoid that corruption. But neither are they "born evil"—destined to become unsavory, irredeemable charlatans. Yes, they have a sin nature and are in need of a Savior, but they are not predisposed to have a bad *character*. Nobility, generosity, integrity—these things are possible for everyone. Although they are not enough for salvation, there is a natural blessing in this world for being faithful to the laws of God, even if they are not recognized as such. In the book of Romans, Paul explained that people who don't know God may still do what is right and so show "the work of the law written in their hearts" (Romans 2:15, KJV). This is an aspect of being born persons. Miss Mason discussed the same thing:

> As for this superior morality of some non-believers, supposing we grant it, what does it amount to? Just to this, that the universe of mind, as the universe of matter, is governed by unwritten laws of God;...that it is possible to ascertain laws and keep laws without recognising the Lawgiver, and that those who do ascertain and keep *any* divine law inherit the blessing due to obedience, whatever be their attitude towards the Lawgiver; just as the man who goes out into blazing sunshine is warmed, though he may shut his eyes and decline to see the sun. Conversely, that they who take no pains to study the principles which govern human action and human thought miss the blessings of obedience to certain laws, though they may inherit the better blessings which come of acknowledged relationship with the Lawgiver. (*Home Education*, p. 39)

Unbelieving people can still have very good characters. If this is possible, there is no reason for believing parents to neglect the possibility of instilling character in their own children. There are principles to guide our efforts, and that is what this principle is about. We parents and teachers must believe we can teach our children to be virtuous and that they are not abandoned to whatever natural tendencies they might have been born with.

Character Is Not Determined at Birth

Miss Mason was an Englishwoman, and English society was dominated by the sense of class and social "place." Some standing was determined by external circumstances. For example, a married woman had a higher place in society than a single one. However, the most significant factor that determined place was birth. Noble birth or humble birth—legitimate birth or illegitimate—a person's birth into society determined his place. The idea of character attached itself to this idea of place. The child of a thief was assumed to have thieving tendencies. The child of a promiscuous woman was assumed to be profligate. A child of a noble family was supposed to be noble, and a gentlemen's child—even if illegitimate—took some pride in that heritage.

These were the attitudes of society at large, illustrated by common tags of wisdom such as "blood will tell" or "what's bred in the bone will come out in the flesh." The popular interest in science, which we have already discussed, seemed to confirm this bias. Genetic traits were inherited—what the parents were, the children would be. Not only were hair color and weak eyesight attributed to heredity but also character traits—good ones or bad ones. Those who believe that outside forces govern us—whether it be the fates or our genes—are embracing *determinism*. By definition, determinism suggests that our lives are determined by something outside of our control and that nothing we can choose or do will make a difference.

The outcome of this kind of thinking, from an educational perspective, is the false assumption that education cannot have an effect on character. Parents might simply abdicate their responsibility if they make these assumptions. If a child is *born* with his character, there is no reason to expend much energy on forming it. Miss Mason opposed that idea and made it a large part of her work both to remind parents of their responsibility and to give them methods to accomplish it.

> If the development of character rather than of faculty is the main work of education, and if people are born, so to speak, ready-made, with all the elements of their after-character in them certain to be developed by time and circumstances, what is left for education to do?...Very commonly, the vote is, do nothing. (*Parents and Children*, p. 73)

Education Is Necessary to Instill Character

The primary purpose of the second principle is to remind us that *doing nothing* is not a good idea. Children need instruction to become the best they can be. If a person is to become virtuous—which is not the same as righteous—there is work for the educator, both parent and teacher. We cannot trust that a child will, by nature alone, grow up into a virtuous person—that is, a person who holds sound principles and lives by them as much as possible. We must find the way to instill the sound principles and offer him the right motivation for following them. When we recall that the two primary principles of education are *children are born persons* and *education is the science of relations*, the task becomes a matter of helping a child to develop a love of virtue.

Miss Mason was not alone in this understanding. For example, John Ruskin wrote:

> The entire object of true education is to make people not merely do the right things, but enjoy the right things—not merely industrious, but to love industry—not merely learned, but to love knowledge—not merely pure, but to love purity—not merely just, but to hunger and thirst after justice. (*The Crown of Wild Olive*, p. 43)

Miss Mason included a hopeful note in this second principle. Children are not born with fixed character—"but with possibilities." If small persons arrive with unformed character that is neither good or bad as yet, the educator—whether parent or teacher—does have an important job to do.

> Here we have the work of education indicated. There are good and evil tendencies in body and mind, heart and soul; and the hope set before us is that we can foster the good so as to attenuate the evil; that is, on condition that we put Education in her true place as the [servant] of Religion. (*Philosophy of Education*, p. 46)

This is work for a lifetime, and eventually each individual becomes responsible for himself. There is a distinction here between what education can do and the role of religion. Our educational work that affects character is only a servant of religion; it does not take the place of a Savior. In these educational principles, Miss Mason's plea to parents and teachers was not to neglect their responsibility to instill virtue. She desired all educators to understand what children need. *Children are born persons*, but they are not born with fully preprogrammed characters; they are dependent on those who nurture them. Parents and teachers may hope to receive help from God, but there is work for them to do:

> I do not undervalue the Divine grace—far otherwise; but we do not always make enough of the fact that Divine grace is exerted on the lines of enlightened human effort; that the parent, for instance, who takes the trouble to understand what he is about

in educating his child, deserves, and assuredly gets, support from above. (*Home Education*, p. 104)

Because Miss Mason felt so strongly about this—that the work of shaping a child's character is the primary work of the educator—she gave us the second principle to highlight the task. When the question of nature and nurture arises, we must remember that nature left to itself will only grow wild. The task of education is to train and cultivate character.

> Nature then, strong as she is, is not invincible; and, at her best, Nature is not to be permitted to ride rampant. Bit and bridle, hand and voice, will get the utmost of endeavour out of her if her training be taken in hand in time; but let Nature run wild, like the forest ponies, and not spur nor whip will break her in. (*Home Education*, p. 104)

That is a rather sobering picture, but it is meant to be a reminder to parents and teachers that the work we do while children are young is especially important. It echoes this injunction: "Train up a child in the way he should go: and when he is old, he will not depart from it" (Proverbs 22:6, KJV). This is a principle, a truth that cannot be circumvented. Children are persons who are "not born either good or bad, but with possibilities for good and for evil." Education is needed to cultivate the character of our children.

🕊

5

Heaven's First Law

Note the order of the movements of the heavenly bodies. The same
law holds good with the whole animal creation. There is also order
in the providence of God.
—C.H. Spurgeon

The Authority Principle Implies Order

Charlotte Mason's third principle seemed to her a natural extension of the first one, *children are born persons*:

> The principles of authority on one hand and obedience on the
> other are natural, necessary, and fundamental. (*Philosophy of
> Education*, p. xxix)

On the face of it, this principle seems to be saying that it is the
job of a parent or teacher to tell children what to do, and it is the
job of children to do it. That is what authority and obedience look
like on the surface. But there is much more to this principle than
a mere veneer of who is giving instructions and who is following
them. This principle implies nothing less than the inherent order of
a universe governed by laws and, by implication, a Lawgiver. Look at
the words she uses—they are not flippant or random. They are deliberately chosen to lay a secure foundation for the work educators are
called to do. These principles are natural. They are necessary. They
are fundamental.

Miss Mason reminded us, "'Order is heaven's first law' and order
is the outcome of authority" (*Philosophy of Education*, p. 69). There are

47

multiple levels of meaning to the concept of order, but the most basic way to understand order is to think of it as the opposite of chaos. If you walk into a room and see LEGO® bricks strewn across the floor with no discernible reason, you can imagine that someone just dumped them out of the box. That's what chaos looks like.

If you walk in and find them sorted into piles of red bricks, blue bricks, black bricks, and white bricks, you may still be dismayed that they are on the floor, but you will *not* suspect that that were dumped out of a box. If you find an elaborately staged model of a castle with figures on the ramparts defending and figures in ranks attacking, you will not think these toys were just poured out onto the floor. If the blocks are laid out in perfectly even rows and columns, covering every bit of available floor space, you may wonder how you will walk across the floor, but you will not think they were simply scattered.

Chaos is lack of order and law. We know chaos when we see it, but in each of the other cases described here, we can perceive that the toys have been arranged according to some law. In one case, they were sorted by the law of color. In another case, they were arranged by the law of a pattern, and in another they were arranged by the law of imagination. When we perceive order, we can usually begin to discern the law that lies behind it. That is what this principle is telling us about the world we live in. Authority and obedience, natural and necessary for society to function, imply order.

Order and Authority Govern Every Aspect of Life

Miss Mason said that without authority, "Society would cease to cohere" (*Philosophy of Education*, p. 69). In the twenty-first century, we feel that an orderly society is slipping away. Miss Mason was able to assume that her culture understood the need for this authority and order. She thought she did not need to elaborate on such foundational truths because "we do not expose the foundations of our house" (*School Education*, preface), but that is less true today. This principle has been rejected, and much popular entertainment speculates upon the idea of what might happen when order collapses entirely. We need to examine what is meant by authority so we can recognize how essential—and inescapable—it is.

Let's start with driving our cars. What if there were no rules about where you could drive? No lanes, signs, or lights to regulate the flow of traffic, no one-way streets or marked parking areas. We have a tendency in our culture to see a lack of authority or rules as the definition of freedom, but what would be the result of this lack of authority in the streets? You might think you'd like the liberty to just drive where you want to go and maybe park on the sidewalk or even in the street in front of your destination, but if everyone else were also driving that way to please themselves, you wouldn't be happy. If ten other cars were parked in the road so that you couldn't get through at all, that would be bad. If you were driving straight through town without stopping and someone else who was driving through town without stopping hit your car, that would be bad. And who would want to be a pedestrian if everyone were driving this way? The authority to make and enforce traffic laws creates order that makes the driving experience better and safer for everyone even when it seems horribly inconvenient or tiresome.

This principle of authority and obedience operates in every aspect of our lives. It is important to understand that the obedience to just authority is honorable—a matter of pride, not slavery. "I've never gotten a traffic ticket in my life" may be spoken with sincere satisfaction by a careful driver who has followed the laws. Soldiers may take pride in carrying out their orders, as did the servants who were still abundant in British society during Miss Mason's lifetime. Even today, we have a service industry, and we can find many waiters, cleaners, mechanics, and others who take pride in doing their job well. Serving well is cause for personal self-esteem. We see this in small children, who are proud when they are able to help. When we think about it rightly, service is a privilege. As Miss Mason pointed out, the higher the authority we serve, the more honorable that service is. Consider the president's cabinet or his closest advisors. Those are offices of service, but because they are serving the president directly, they are highly prized. Miss Mason explained it this way:

> We want to be governed: servants like to receive their "orders";
> soldiers and schoolboys enjoy discipline; there is satisfaction in
> stringent Court etiquette; the fact of being "under orders" adds
> dignity to character. (*Philosophy of Education*, p. 335)

If we have no other authority than ourselves, we may imagine that we are simply following our destiny—because it is in our nature *as persons* to want to submit to a worthy authority. When necessary, we are also naturally able to exercise authority. We consider it a matter of honor or trust. Can you chair the meeting? Will you take charge of refreshments? Organize a prayer chain? Most of us recognize that the exercise of authority is also a form of service—one that carries heavier responsibility. Parents and teachers have authority in our roles, but we are also serving—serving a higher authority.

Sometimes authority is earned by virtue of knowledge. An authority on antiques can tell you if your object is old and valuable, or just old. An authority on electricity can tell you whether or not your house has been wired correctly. A handwriting authority can discern whether a signature is authentic. More often, authority is not grounded in knowledge but is rather derived from an office, a position. The president of a company makes decisions and gives orders because he has been entrusted with that authority. Locally elected authorities create statutes that local residents must abide by. Higher offices make decisions and laws that a whole nation must accept. In the home, parents are given authority over children. This is natural authority, and we must have it, or society would be reduced to chaos.

Moral Authority Safeguards Us from Power Struggles

Many people would accept authority as necessary at this level, but there is also the question of higher authority—a moral authority—and Miss Mason's third principle is primarily concerned with moral authority. Without a higher law—a moral compass that indicates whether something is right or wrong—there are no principles to limit the authority of individuals who hold it. Used incorrectly, authority may be arbitrary, recognizing no law but strength, and it can degenerate into tyranny.

Right and wrong are concepts that our culture does not want to recognize. Everything is supposed to be relative: What is right for you might not be right for me; conversely, what you think is wrong might be right for me. Where is the authority that can tell us? Our culture says, "There is no such authority." Many people refuse to acknowledge anyone's right to tell them what they can do. We speak of truth as relative—your truth and my truth, but never absolute—The Truth. I have read denials that two plus two must equal four—because even mathematical truths are not allowed to stand unchallenged.

Our culture resents authority, although we cannot avoid it. When we attempt to reject natural authority, the only thing left is power and force. Legitimate authority is replaced by power—those who have the power will impose their authority on those who are weaker. However, force is not the same thing as natural authority, and Miss Mason wanted the principle of natural moral authority in the world to have a prominent place in our understanding of what it means to be a person. She reminded us that this is a natural law from which we cannot escape. Underlying her philosophy was "the recognition of authority as a fundamental principle, as universal and as inevitable in the moral world as is that of gravitation in the physical" (*School Education*, p. 126). We are persons who owe obedience to authority, and this allows us to live in peace and order rather than in chaos:

> To dream of liberty, in the sense of every man his own sole governor, is as futile as to dream of a world in which apples do not necessarily drop from the tree, but may fly off at a tangent in any direction. (*School Education*, p. 10)

This is the way that natural principles, which are the laws of the universe, work. Just as you could perceive the laws that governed the toys on the floor, you can perceive the law of gravity. Isaac Newton is famous for it. A careful examination of the world and the way it must operate reveals the principle of authority and obedience. Like gravity, the influence of this law is irresistible. If we try to ignore it, we may get hurt. When authority is eroded and chaos overtakes society, lawlessness rules. If there are no absolute moral rules to govern the governors, what authority can we appeal to? When we acknowledge no legitimate authority, the question of who will rule becomes a power struggle.

A culture that will not believe in order must accept chaos. Principles determine behavior, and this is true on a wide scale as well as on an individual one. A culture that denies order and authority and embraces the chaos of relativism will act accordingly, and thus we have a world in which no one is supposed to be obliged to do anything they do not want to do or hear anything they disagree with. If we want to accomplish the character-forming objectives of education in the lives of our children, we need to know what the laws of education are and act accordingly. *Children are born persons* who live in an ordered universe that tells us what virtue and morality should be.

Authority Implies Duty

Authority carries within it the seeds of duty and obligation. If there are traffic laws, we must obey them or pay penalties. If there is a moral authority, it implies that we have certain obligations—we ought to do certain things and abstain from certain other things simply because our moral authority has declared what is right and what is wrong. Miss Mason was explicit that the authority principle is dealing with moral authority:

> Let us consider the principle of authority, which is the basis of moral as it is of religious teaching. "Ought" is part of the verb "to owe," and that which we owe is a personal debt to a Lawgiver and Ruler, however men name the final authority. If they choose to speak of Buddha or Humanity, they do not escape from the sense of a moral authority. They know that that which they *ought* is that which they owe to do, a debt to some power or personality external to themselves. God has made us so that, however much we may be in the dark as to the divine Name, we can never for a minute escape from the sense of "Ought." (*School Education*, pp. 126–27)

Miss Mason recognized that there is no escape from the sense of obligation we have to obey authority. If we don't acknowledge God as the Lawgiver, we may invoke environmentalism or social justice or human rights as our authority, but we will seek some order, some authority, to govern our conduct. Miss Mason included in her educational principles the moral authority of God in the world that requires an orderly framework.

If you want a real, character-forming education, it must be conducted under conditions as they are. We must discern the reality that is true and universal and fundamental—the laws of education that exist and may be discovered, just as we can discern the law that governs the toys on the floor. The authority and obedience mentioned in Miss Mason's third principle refer only incidentally to the teacher/ pupil or parent/child relationships. This principle addresses a much larger concept.

The existence of authority provides us with the fundamental idea of *duty*—of *ought*: There are things that we should do, ought to do, must do. The chosen motto for the PNEU was "I am, I can, I ought, I will." The principles are embedded in this motto. You can see that "I am" and "I can" are the result of the first principle—*children are born persons*. A person is self-existing and has the power to act (for good or evil, as stated in the second principle)—that is what it means to be a person. But "I ought" is a reference to this authority principle and implies an obligation—the existence of an ordered world in which there is a Lawgiver and there are laws that a person is duty-bound to obey. This is implied by the principle that authority and obedience are *natural* and *necessary*.

This principle is also *fundamental* because the whole purpose for the character-forming education demanded by the second principle lies upon the moral authority of this third principle. If it does not matter what kind of character a person has—if we cannot say that people *should* be honest and industrious and *ought* to show consideration and care for others, then we have no real grounds for teaching children these things. They might as well act purely in their own self-interests. However, because there is a moral authority that gives us a standard, we must educate our children in virtue.

Order Implies Meaning

Regardless of what our culture is telling us, we do not live in a world of meaningless chaos. When we acknowledge the order that is inherent in the universe, it implies meaning. Order is heaven's first law. When we perceive order, even if we don't fully understand it, we feel the pull—like the irresistible pull of gravity—to seek out the Truth and meaning that we know must be there. Order means something. Just as the toys on the floor had been placed with purpose, order must have a cause. Because we are persons, we are so made that we want and need to know what—and Who—it is.

In the twenty-first century, we need to understand this principle just as much as we need to understand that a person is not a machine.

Even those who do not believe in God are governed by the sense of *ought* because it is in our nature to desire authority and meaning.

If we do not acknowledge the God of the Bible, we seek meaning and authority elsewhere. In earlier cultures, people made gods of the things they could see—mountains, stars, even cows or beetles. The Egyptians worshipped the sun and the Nile River. The ancient Greeks and Romans made gods that were like themselves—supermen and superwomen with power and authority over their individual realms. Neptune was a god-man who ruled the sea and Venus the goddess who ruled the heart. Today, we make gods of things like money. Economic success is the highest good, and therefore we "ought" to go to college because we "should" get a good job and earn more money.

This principle is meant to remind us that not only are children under authority, but teachers and parents are as well. We have obligations that arise because we have been given the authority of an office. We may not be autocrats or tyrants; we may not order things to please ourselves without considering the moral laws of education and learning in both academics and child rearing.

Miss Mason lived in a culture that took certain truths for granted. We are not able to do that, and if we want this aspect of education to have its proper role, we need to be more explicit than she needed to be. There is order in the world. There is authority. There is right and wrong. There is such a thing as absolute truth. If we reject that concept, education can only flounder, along with all the other aspects of our culture. If we reject the notion that there are absolute truths that govern the way children learn and grow, educational methods become a tool in a power struggle. Educational fads are imposed on us by those who have the power either to compel us by law or to persuade us by marketing.

Because we are persons, we desire order and meaning. Our efforts in education will not feel futile or chaotic when we know that we are working in conjunction with the laws that have been established for learning. *Children are born persons* and *education is the science of relations.* When those principles guide our actions, we will feel the confidence that comes from acting in obedience to authority.

Our Duty Is Service to a King

The final duty for all of us is to learn to rule *ourselves*, not by doing whatever we please but by choosing to serve just authority. It is an honorable calling to live in accordance with moral law. Our knowledge of what is right, not our natural desires, should govern our choices. We can learn to rejoice in doing our duty because everything we do is in the service of a great King.

One of the only verses in the Bible addressed to children explains to them their role in the natural order of the world: "Children obey your parents in the Lord, for this is right" (Ephesians 6:1, KJV). That simple injunction implies the authority and order of the universe—God is the original authority who has invested parents with authority over children and laid upon children the moral *ought* that should compel them for no other reason than the moral authority itself: because it is right. Children and parents alike can find joy in obedience:

> There are, in this poor stuff we call human nature, founts of loyalty, worship, passionate devotion, glad service, which have, alas! to be unsealed in the earth-laden older heart, but only ask place to flow from the child's. There is no safeguard and no joy like that of being under orders, being possessed, controlled, continually in the service of One whom it is gladness to obey.
>
> We lose sight of the fact in our modern civilisation, but a king, a leader, implies warfare, a foe, victory—possible defeat and disgrace. And this is the conception of life which cannot too soon be brought before children. (*Parents and Children*, p. 57)

When we delve into all that the third principle means, we are able to lift our heads and bear our responsibilities as parents and teachers with honor because we know we are serving a higher calling. When we teach children the laws and principles of the world—when we teach *according* to the laws and principles in our world—we are celebrating the order that is in the universe and shouldering our share of the work that belongs to it. We are doing what we ought to do. As we move on to the next principle, we will see that one of the things we owe to our children is due respect as persons.

6

Due Respect

God said, Let us make man in our image.
—Genesis 1:26, KJV

Authority Is Limited by Respect for Personhood

Charlotte Mason made her point about the existence of authority in part so that she could remind us there is a limitation to the educational authority of a parent or teacher. When we fully appreciate the nature of an ordered universe, we can see our position as parents or teachers as part of an ordered whole. An educator, too, is under authority and must act according to the principles—the most important of which is that *children are born persons*. Because each child is a person, our authority should not be arbitrary but should be tempered by the respect due a person. No authority gives us the right to trespass upon the personhood of a child. The fourth principle says we must remember that the personality of a child "must not be encroached upon, whether by the direct use of fear or love, suggestion or influence, or by undue play upon any one natural desire" (*Philosophy of Education*, p. xxix).

The primary application of this principle lies in the ways that we motivate children to learn. They can be motivated by love of a teacher or parent who subtly urges, "Learn this so that I will be proud of you." They can be motivated by fear: "Memorize this or face the unpleasant consequences." They can be motivated by any of the natural desires that are common to all—for acclaim, distinction, or rewards—but

57

when these are overused, they encroach upon the personhood of a child.

Two primary principles—*children are born persons* and *education is the science of relations*—influence the ways in which we motivate our students. Persons have a natural desire—curiosity—to form relationships with knowledge of all kinds. If our teaching invokes motives that hinder the natural development of those relations, we are infringing on their personhood.

Remember that the code of education in the Gospels is essentially negative in character:

> Have we considered that…the rules we receive for the bringing up of children are for the most part negative? We may not despise them, or hinder them, ("suffer little children"), or offend them by our brutish clumsiness of action and want of serious thought. (*Philosophy of Education*, pp. 80–81)

We might say rather bluntly that we are not permitted to brainwash children. Miss Mason reminded us that although we as educators represent a certain kind of authority, we are not the ultimate authority. We, too, must submit to our duties and obligations, including the duty to respect the personhood of a child. We owe them some serious thought about the principles we use to educate them, both in the academic realm and in the matter of child-rearing.

Wrong Motivations Undermine Personhood

We do not have the right to make children do something by any means at all. We should not use either fear or love to force a child. We cannot resort to our personal influence—which is little more than imposing our personality on theirs. We must not use psychological tricks such as "suggestion" to make children learn something or behave as we want them to. Miss Mason lived in the age when psychology was emerging as a science. Suggestion and hypnotism went hand in hand, but this mention of suggestion in the fourth principle is probably just a hint that all kinds of psychological manipulation are inappropriate methods in education. This is an educational principle and must be understood in that context.

It is easier to understand these adjunct principles when we understand the primary principles well. If a child is a person with a natural desire to know all about the world, including a natural desire to know God, any method we use to educate is either helping or hindering the relationship-building process. If our primary objective in education is the formation of character and strengthening of virtue, as the second principle suggests, then that objective carries more weight than learning phonics or subtraction facts. We are not free to compel children to learn either academics or virtue by hook or by crook. We must teach, but we must comprehend our boundaries. This is not a hindrance to the work of the educator. When we understand a principle well we act upon it naturally, and everything falls into place.

> All action comes out of the ideas we hold and if we ponder duly upon personality we shall come to perceive that we cannot commit a greater offence than to maim or crush, or subvert any part of a person. (*Philosophy of Education*, p. 80)

Some of what Miss Mason said on this subject is not entirely relevant for us. For example, she spoke of a schoolgirl developing a crush on a beloved teacher and slavishly acting to please that teacher. I think we are less likely to see that sort of thing today, but the principle does not change. We simply have to examine the way it operates within our current climate.

Do you toss your litter in the trash because you'll be fined if you toss it on the ground or because it's right to care for the environment? Do you abstain from siphoning your neighbor's gasoline because you're afraid of being caught or because you know it's wrong to steal? Do you attend church on Sunday because you're afraid God will be angry if you don't or because you truly desire to worship with other believers and want to learn and grow? What are your motivations for doing the things you do?

You can ask similar questions about the ways you are motivating your children. Are your children doing their schoolwork only because they'll be punished if they don't? Are they pleasant only because their allowance will be docked for arguing? If artificial motivations are used instead of right and natural ones, children may learn to value cheap rewards like stickers and pizza parties—or even grades—over knowledge itself.

The Right Motive Should Not Be Hindered

The point Miss Mason is making with her prohibition of things like fear and influence is simply by way of reminding us that we are undermining the real work of education—to form a child's character—by the use of any artificial motive or even by leaning too heavily on natural motivations. For example, rewards are very motivating, but if we excessively use rewards to motivate children to learn or to behave rightly, we are actually hindering their character development. A child who always tells the truth is not a virtuous, honest child if she simply fears punishment for lying. A child who sits quietly during a Sunday School lesson for the sake of getting a piece of candy when it is over is not developing good character. We do not have the liberty to trick children into the obedience required by the authority principle.

> If the parent realise that...he is the appointed agent to train the child up to the intelligent obedience of the self-compelling, law-abiding human being, he will see that he has no right to *forego* the obedience of his child....Also, he will see that the motive of the child's obedience is not the arbitrary one of, "Do this, or that, because I have said so," but the motive of the apostolic injunction, "Children, obey your parents in the Lord, *for this is right*." (*Home Education*, p. 161)

If children are going to develop the right relations with the virtues we want to incorporate in their lives, they must be motivated for the right reason. They need to learn to love doing right and to love doing their duty simply because they are compelled by the *ought* of moral authority. The scriptural instruction to children offers no reason for obeying other than "for this is right." It is all too easy for educators to fall back on artificial motivators to achieve desired behavior, but because this is a hindrance to the real objective of education, we must use caution. We want our children to choose to do the right things because they are right and because they care about doing what is right. No one can be motivated by that reason alone unless they are given the chance and no other motives—reward or punishment—are substituted.

When we try to entice our children to learn math or eat vegetables by offering prizes, we are subtly telling them that the thing we want them to do is distasteful. A child knows that no one ever has to coax him to eat cake or candy. He likes them, and they are their own reward. Difficult as it is, we must remember that the same thing is true of knowledge and virtue. They are their own rewards. It may take a child a little longer to find that out for himself, but we hinder that process when we intervene by playing upon other desires.

Children Must Be Motivated as Persons

I once viewed some instructional material intended for teachers. It showed a picture of a donkey pulling a cart and illustrated how the donkey could be made to do his work by a carrot or a stick—by reward or threat. The material was suggesting that it was better to motivate by carrots than sticks, but the fundamental illustration is profoundly flawed because *children are not donkeys.* The donkey doesn't want to pull the cart and has no reason to submit to the will of the cart-owner other than the use of external rewards or threats. But *children are born persons.*

Because they are persons, they possess certain natural desires that are common to everyone. They actually do have within them a desire to learn and know and a desire to do what is right. As parents and teachers, we are in a position of authority that allows us to motivate children to learn. However, we are also responsible to educate ourselves about the best and most effective ways to do that—ways that do not demean people by training them like a donkey or a robot or a puppet or a pet or like anything other than a person.

As we apprehend and appreciate each principle in full, we begin to see how they fit together. As a whole, these educational principles expand our comprehension of how a person should be educated. Our understanding should take the form of actions that will make our efforts effective. A clear understanding of the fourth principle will naturally eliminate artificial motives from our educational methods and allow the strong natural motivation children have—curiosity and a desire to know—to develop freely. The result will be a healthy, robust learning environment in which children—persons made in the image of God—can flourish.

7

A Spiritual Octopus

The human mind is so complex and things are so tangled up with
each other that, to explain a blade of straw, one would have to take
to pieces an entire universe.
—Remy de Gourmont

There Are Two Analogies for the Mind of a Person

I hope it is becoming clearer that the principles which follow the
first principle are meant to amplify the statement that *children are
born persons*. That declaration is a primary one—one of the vital principles that govern everything an educator should be thinking about.
Following that up with "they are not born good or bad, but with possibilities" focuses our attention on the primary role of education—to
form the character of our students in a way that will result in virtuous living. The principle of authority and obedience reminds us that
we are doing this because there is an order in the world and this task
is our duty. Children in turn have their duties to fulfill, and only thus
does the world go on and society cohere. If we want the learning
process to remain unadulterated, we are obligated not to introduce
false motivation or trick children into outwardly correct behavior
without the proper inward motivation. All of these principles grow
out of our essential understanding of what a person is and what a
person ought to do and be.

Principles nine, ten, and eleven focus our attention on the concept
of mind—that aspect of a person which education must address.
Because we cannot dissect a person, remove his mind, and examine it

under a microscope nor subject it to analysis by X-ray or MRI or any other device we possess, we must fall back on analogies to help us understand what a mind is and what a person who has a mind needs.

Throughout the centuries, two kinds of analogies about the way the mind learns have been offered to us. One analogy suggests that the mind is some kind of receptacle—a bucket, a vessel, a blank slate, or empty shelves. It is an emptiness that must be filled, and the implication is that it will be filled with information. John Locke popularized the concept of the blank slate—a *tabula rasa*—and his ideas persist in many of our pedagogical practices, although few educators would consciously accept his "blank slate" view of children.

There is a better alternative to the empty vessel analogy. Rather than considering the mind a receptacle to be filled, we may view it as a vital force that requires energizing fuel. It's not difficult to find this inspirational quote: "Education is not the filling of a bucket but the lighting of a fire." Plutarch, William Butler Yeats, and more are credited with expressing variations of this perspective.

Others have made similar observations—that the education of the mind is represented by fueling an organism. In *On Christian Doctrine*, Augustine wrote that there is an analogy between learning and eating. In his essay "Of the Education of Children," Montaigne reminded us that excellent books provide material for the mind to feed upon and digest. They understood that the mind is a living entity that requires sustenance.

In these analogies, the fire requires wood to burn, and the body requires food to live and grow; in education, the mind must be fueled or fed with its proper food. Charlotte Mason made these analogies part of the principles to help us understand the nature of the work we are called to do.

Our Analogy of Mind Provides Perspective

Miss Mason was aware that the mind of a person was the primary instrument of education. She rejected the idea that it is a receptacle—a "sac." She called the mind a "living organism" that needs to be fed. The ninth principle states:

> We hold that the child's mind is no mere sac to hold ideas; but is rather, if the figure may be allowed, a spiritual organism, with an

appetite for all knowledge. This is its proper diet, with which it is prepared to deal; and which it can digest and assimilate as the body does foodstuffs. (*Philosophy of Education*, p. xxx)

In the tenth principle, Miss Mason tackles one educational philosopher's faulty ideas about the mind:

Such a doctrine as *e.g.* the Herbartian, that the mind is a receptacle, lays the stress of Education (the preparation of knowledge in enticing morsels duly offered) upon the teacher. (*Philosophy of Education*, p. xxx)

I have been puzzled by the inclusion of one particular person's ideas in the principles. Most of these educational principles are timeless and represent universal truths, while this one feels dated—relevant to nineteenth- or early twentieth-century Britain, but not as relevant today. Almost no one who hasn't read Charlotte Mason's volumes will ever have heard of Johann Friedrich Herbart, so there seems to be little point in mentioning him.

However, we can learn something from the fact that she did mention him. We too must address the universal principles to the ideas of our own time. The ideas of Herbart are not especially current, but he is offered merely as a bad example. We have our own examples of faulty thinking that need to be addressed, either for the same reason or for other reasons. If we know the universal principles well and can recognize them when they are discussed in any terms, we can spot the aberrations, the false steps, the untenable ideas that undermine the primary working of those principles.

For example, one popular trend in education is to emphasize "STEM" subjects to such a degree that science, technology, engineering, and math dominate a child's school career. There is nothing wrong with those studies, but if a child has no time to read poetry and stories, to experience art and music, to delve into history and learn to appreciate the heritage of the past, we have violated the principle that *education is the science of relations.* A person wants to know about many things, and a child needs a broad exposure to all kinds of knowledge, especially in the younger years. That wide exposure lays a good foundation for specializing later—in a STEM subject or anything else.

Our Analogy of Mind Governs Our Priorities and Practices

The practical educational point of this group of principles is made in the eleventh principle, and it concerns the nature of what we must offer to children. If their minds were simply receptacles to be filled, then facts—information or data—would be adequate educational matter. But because the mind is not a receptacle but rather a vital force that requires energy, it requires something more sustaining. Mere facts will not satisfy a living mind—it cannot thrive upon bits of information such as the fact that Tallahassee is the capital of Florida or the Amazonian jungle covers so many square miles. In *Hard Times*, Charles Dickens illustrated this soul-killing kind of education in the schoolmaster Gradgrind. In her eleventh principle, Miss Mason asserted:

> We, believing that the normal child has powers of mind which fit him to deal with all knowledge proper to him, give him a full and generous curriculum; taking care only that all knowledge offered him is vital, that is, *that facts are not presented without their informing ideas.* (*Philosophy of Education*, p. xxx, emphasis added)

The mind requires more than facts—it needs *ideas*. This truth about education has shaped its history across the centuries. Ideas are living in the way that seeds are living—they contain the power to grow and produce a harvest everywhere they are planted. They contain within them the energy to produce new lines of thought under the proper conditions. Samuel Taylor Coleridge, one of the thinkers who influenced Miss Mason, wrote, "From the first or initiative idea, as from a seed, successive ideas germinate" (*Philosophy of Education*, p. 107). Miss Mason's own writing is filled with examples of the power of ideas in the mind of a person.

> What is an idea? we ask, and find ourselves plunged beyond our depth. A live thing of the mind, seems to be the conclusion of our greatest thinkers from Plato to Bacon, from Bacon to Coleridge. We all know how an idea *"strikes," "seizes," "catches hold of," "impresses"* us and at last, if it be big enough, *"possesses"* us; in a word, behaves like an entity.
>
> If we enquire into any person's habits of life, mental preoccupation, devotion to a cause or pursuit, he will usually tell us that

such and such *an idea struck him.* This potency of an idea is matter of common recognition. No phrase is more common and more promising than, "I have an idea." (*Philosophy of Education*, p. 105)

In many ways, this is not how we are accustomed to think of education. Most of us have been deeply affected by our own exposure to institutional schools and modern pedagogies that prevail even in Sunday School classrooms. We tend to view education as the mastery of some specific content or material, but underlying that view of education is the analogy that the mind is a receptacle.

If you go to the cupboard looking for sugar and the sugar is there, the cupboard is functioning as it should. If you ask a question and a child can produce the correct answer, you might assume that education was successful. The child "learned" the correct answer to the question. But what if that is entirely the wrong picture, and education is not about producing correct answers to dreary questions? What if the mind is a hungry, living entity and not a receptacle at all? The cupboard is unaffected and unchanged by the presence of the sugar and other items within. It produces them upon request, but it remains exactly as it was before. So it is with children who dutifully produce the right answers but are unmoved by what they know. If education is meant to produce change and growth in the learner, we need a different working analogy.

Faith Is Required to Act upon an Idea

Miss Mason rejected the receptacle view of mind and embraced the analogy that the mind is a living, spiritual entity that is hungry and must be fed in order to grow and thrive. Mere data will not satisfy that hunger:

> The mind is a spiritual octopus, reaching out limbs in every direction to draw in enormous rations of that which under the action of the mind itself becomes knowledge. Nothing can stale its infinite variety; the heavens and the earth, the past, the present, and future, things great and things minute, nations and men, the universe, all are within the scope of the human intelligence. (*Philosophy of Education*, p. 330)

If we join Miss Mason in this view, we will find ourselves needing to rethink the whole process of education as we understand it. This is a radical paradigm shift, and it does not come easily. What will education look like if we abandon the apparatus of textbooks and grades and weekly quizzes and tests? What happens when we abandon measuring every incremental accumulation of information and calling that education? What if we truly embraced this principle and believed in mind, as Miss Mason called us to do? "Believe in mind," she said, and believing in mind means acknowledging the nature of a mind and what it truly needs. Miss Mason was confident about the proper fuel:

> The mind, in fact, requires sustenance—as does the body, in order that it increase and be strong; but because the mind is not to be measured or weighed but is spiritual, so its sustenance must be spiritual too, must, in fact, be ideas. (*Philosophy of Education*, p. 10)

This is not an educational principle you can have a mere nodding acquaintance with. If it is going to become your own principle that you embrace and work out in your educational practices, it will require some thinking and pondering. A paradigm shift is not a box to be checked off. Educational materials abound—all the trappings of workbooks and curriculums and assessments and rubrics vie for attention. With this principle, Miss Mason is sweeping it all aside without a moment's regret in favor of the thing that will truly nourish the mind of a learner and make a difference in his life:

> We know that food is to the body what fuel is to the steam-engine, the sole source of energy; once we realise that the mind too works only as it is fed education will appear to us in a new light. The body pines and develops humours upon tabloids [vitamin tablets] and other food substitutes.... The mind is capable of dealing with only one kind of food; it lives, grows and is nourished upon ideas only; mere information is to it as a meal of sawdust to the body; there are no organs for the assimilation of the one more than of the other. (*Philosophy of Education*, pp. 104–5)

It is one of the great tragedies of modern education that many of us have been offered nothing but sawdust and other inadequate substitutes for real knowledge and ideas. However, if we have confidence in these principles, we have it within our power to do better both for our children and for ourselves. It's never too late to begin learning—a process that is meant to continue for all our lives. Our minds will be sustained and grow stronger only if they are well fed upon living ideas. If we believe this, it will revolutionize our approach to education.

8

Know Thyself

No one person should be launched upon life without an ordered
knowledge of himself.
—Charlotte Mason, *Formation of Character*

A Relationship with Personhood

The Primary Principles Are Related to Each Other

Before we go further, I want to return to the two vital, primary principles. *Education is the science of relations* has a long history in the tradition of education. Plato wrote in his *Laws*:

> There is one element you could isolate in any account you give [of education], and this is the correct formation of our feelings of pleasure and pain, which makes us hate what we ought to hate from first to last, and love what we ought to love. Call this "education," and I, at any rate, think you would be giving it its proper name.

Augustine wrote about *ordering the affections*, or learning to care properly about the things that matter most. We've already observed that John Ruskin saw education as learning to love virtue. Charlotte Mason, of course, recognized this concept as one of the most vital principles of education—something that should shape and drive all of our educational practices.

When *education is the science of relations* is paired with *children are born persons*, a very particular relationship emerges. Imagine a Venn

71

diagram, in which two circles partially overlap, creating an intersecting third category that incorporates both of the original ones. That is what happens when we place *education is the science of relations* next to *children are born persons*. We create an overlapping category that represents the *relationship* of a person with what it means to *be* a person—the relationship of a person with personhood itself.

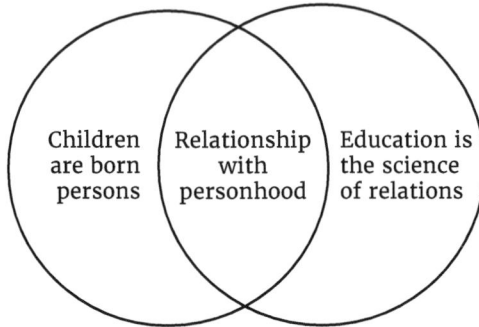

A Person Needs to Understand Personhood

Please take a moment to understand this idea. *Children are born persons*, certainly, but they are not born with a full understanding of what a person *is*. *Education is the science of relations* reminds us that children have a right to develop a relationship with all areas of knowledge. They have a right, even a responsibility, to develop a relationship with the full concept of personhood. What is a person? What powers are present in a person? What obligations does a person have and what privileges? This, too, is a relation to be developed, and it is succinctly expressed by the oracular injunction given to Socrates: Know thyself.

It is no accident that Miss Mason referenced that advice in her catechism of education and told us:

> It is time we reverted to the teaching of Socrates. "Know thyself," exhorted the wise man, in season and out of season; and it will be well with us when we understand that to acquaint a child with himself—what he is as a human being—is a great part of education. (*Parents and Children*, p. 242)

A person should have a firm relationship with personhood, and Miss Mason's twenty principles do not leave us to wonder what it is that we need to know. Principles sixteen, seventeen, eighteen, and nineteen—four of the twenty—give us a framework for developing a relationship with our personhood. In chapter 1, I mentioned that in the beginning of her first book, Miss Mason drew attention to the two primary principles, and after mentioning *children are born persons* and *education is the science of relations*, she told us, "Add to this one or two keys to self knowledge." The sixteenth principle tells us exactly what those keys are:

> There are two guides to moral and intellectual self-management
> to offer to children, which we may call "the way of the will" and
> "the way of the reason." (*Philosophy of Education*, p. xxxi)

We often use the shorthand "way of the will" and "way of reason," as Miss Mason did, but these principles contain a breadth of ideas that we need to explore in a way that makes sense to us today in the twenty-first century. If these ideas lie at the intersection of the two most important principles, their significance is elevated beyond what we might guess by looking at the numbers assigned to them. They come late on the list, but they are not less important because of that. They are the connection or relationship between the two primary principles.

A Person Possesses a Will

Making Choices Is a Human Privilege

Will and *reason* are the two characteristics that set a person apart from all other creatures. In our tendency to use technology to describe ourselves, we often hear of DNA being compared to a computer program—data that determines many things and drives our behavior. We see this in the animal world. Beavers and fish build the kinds of homes their instincts drive them to build. Birds build nests as they have always built them. Lions hunt for food, while their prey grazes. Spiders build webs to capture their food, and jellyfish drift on the waves, waiting for food to come within reach of floating tentacles. None of them makes a choice. They behave as they must. Only people are different because we can choose.

Notice the point—we *can* choose—but we don't have to. It is possible to simply live in accordance with the people and world around us—to wear what everybody wears, read what everybody reads, and think what everybody seems to think. But it is the distinction of a person to choose—to *will* in an active way—to make *conscious* choices. This is the reason that using improper motivation undermines the personhood of a child—it interferes with the development of his own will to choose to do right. Miss Mason said that just as a king must reign, so must a man *will* [choose], and if he drifts like a jellyfish, ingesting the opinions of others, he is not fulfilling his responsibility as a person. She wrote:

> Thus far we have seen, that, just as to reign is the distinctive quality of a king, so is to *will* the quality of a man. A king is not a king unless he reign; and a man is less than a man unless he *will*.
>
> Further, we have seen that we have the choice of willing or not willing. It is even possible to go through life without an act of will. (Charlotte Mason, *Ourselves*, Book II, p. 140)

Our Will Responds to Our Duty

If we remember that part of being a person means we live in a world of order and authority, which implies an *ought*—a duty that is laid upon us—we begin to see the function of the will. The will of a man must answer to the *ought* that is before him and *choose* to do his duty. This principle, which lies at the intersection of the two primary principles, helps to anchor a child in his place in the order of the universe and is founded on having the right motivation behind the choices he makes. The principles do indeed work together in vital harmony, as Miss Mason showed us:

> It is only in proportion as the will of the child is in the act of obedience, and he obeys because his sense of *right* makes him *desire* to obey in spite of temptations to disobedience—not of constraint, but willingly—that the habit has been formed which will, hereafter, enable the child to use the strength of his will against his inclinations when these prompt him to lawless courses. (*Home Education*, pp. 161–62)

She also reminded us that the will can only operate in favor of something external to ourselves. If we act according to our inclinations, in our own self-interest, we are acting according to some of the many natural desires or "appetites" that make up our self. No act of will makes us eat—hunger drives that. We sleep or rest because we are weary. We get up and go to work for the sake of a paycheck. We buy the food that tastes good or the clothes that are popular. It is possible to drift through life—wafted by our own inclinations or the stronger influence of others—without a single act of will, but that is a shame and represents a failure to fully comprehend what it means to be a person.

You are a person and can choose, and if you are wise, you will use your will to act for the sake of something you care about. That's why the full development of our proper relations in all spheres is so vital. Will must exercise itself in service or obedience to something *outside* of the self and its appetites. Thus we have the mother who gets up in exhaustion to care for her crying infant, the man who works long hours and sacrifices his free time to provide for his family, or the soldier who puts himself in danger to rescue an injured comrade. When personal, selfish *wants* are suppressed or denied for the sake of another person, or even for the sake of a cause or an idea, it is because the *will* is in operation. When we love others or country or truth or honor or God, we can suppress our personal desires and choose to act on behalf of others. Not everyone who looks successful by worldly standards has learned this truth. Miss Mason explained:

> It is not safe to take success in life as a criterion. His Will is the measure of the man; and many a man has become rich or famous without willing, on the easy lines of his nature, by the strength of his desires while many another of constant will lives unknown and yet it is the persons of constant will, which implies impersonal aims, who are the world's great possession, and are discerned to be such. (*Ourselves*, Book II, p. 132)

One of the key things an educator must do is to help a child become a person who is able to use his will. In her book *Minds More Awake*, Anne White noted its central importance:

> I've become convinced that the Way of the Will is, in fact, the Start Here point on Charlotte Mason's map. It is Christian's Wicket Gate in *Pilgrim's Progress*, Lucy's Lamp Post in Narnia. (p. 18)

Distinguish between Will and Willfulness

Miss Mason urged us not to embrace the fallacy that *willfulness* is the same as *will*—that a child who cries when he cannot have what he merely *wants* has a "strong will." This is not so. Rather, he is driven by his personal desires and stubbornly refuses to relinquish what he wants (not wills). The child who can stop crying when he told to is the child who has a strong will, because he can make himself do something because it is right. The idea that you can "make yourself" do what you ought to do is the essence of will. This is something that a person needs to understand about himself, and Christ is our example. He illustrated for us that willfulness is rebellion against the order and authority God has placed in the world.

> It has been well observed that each of the three recorded temptations of our Lord in the wilderness is a suggestion, not of an act of overt sin, but of an act of *willfulness*, that state directly opposed to obedience, and out of which springs all that foolishness which is bound up in the heart of a child. (*Home Education*, p. 161)

As we educate our children, it is just this concept we want to convey to them—that they are persons who live in an ordered world under proper authority, and therefore they are doing their duty when they learn to make themselves do what is right. The person who chooses to do right because it is right, not for any artificial reason, has a noble and virtuous character—the very thing we hope to see established in the lives of our young people. Being able to rule yourself is the mark of a mature person.

Exercising our wills to choose what is right is, in fact, very hard. Anyone who has tried to diet knows that "will power" is real, but it is also finite. Sooner or later, you come to the end of it. Your will has exhausted itself, and the likelihood that you will give in to temptation and be ruled by your appetite is very great. The same holds true of other temptations to do what we know we *ought* not—our will can sustain us and keep us making the right choices...until it fails. Romans chapter seven is Paul's familiar lament that he does want to do the right things, but his ability to do them is hampered by his own fallible human nature.

Sometimes Our Wills Need to Rest

Miss Mason had a specific suggestion for how to deal with this weakness in will. This is what she actually meant by "the way of the will." Because the will is finite, it cannot resist our wants indefinitely. But it is distractible. Rather than stand in front of a temptation and resist it face to face, we can mentally run off and do something else. Miss Mason called it "diversion" and referred to the Latin origin of the word, which means a change of course.

If your will is getting tired, she said, think about something else—something quite different, and the more attractive and interesting to you, the better. She suggested thinking about a planned purchase or an interesting event on the horizon. You could also read an engaging book, make plans for a friend's birthday, or organize your Christmas baking. The idea is simply to change your thoughts and give your will a rest so that it remains strong enough to keep you from doing what you have chosen not to do.

> It is something to *know* what to do with ourselves when we are beset, and the knowledge of this *way of the will* is so far the secret of a happy life, that it is well worth imparting to the children. Are you cross? Change your thoughts. Are you tired of trying? Change your thoughts. Are you craving for things you are not to have? Change your thoughts; there is a power within you, your own will, which will enable you to turn your attention from thoughts that make you unhappy *and wrong*, to thoughts that make you happy *and right*. And this is the exceedingly simple way in which the will acts; this is the sole secret of the power over himself which the strong man wields—he can compel himself to think of what he chooses, and *will* not allow himself in thoughts that breed mischief. (*Home Education*, pp. 325–26)

Bearing in mind that the object of education is character formation, this understanding of the will is a powerful tool. Even quite small children can begin to appreciate the power that they have to make themselves behave—to rule their own small persons. They need not be the slaves of willfulness (doing what they *want* rather than willfully choosing what is right) because they have encountered the authority of duty—of *ought*. They can take pride in fulfilling their

obligations, whether they must pick up toys or resist touching something forbidden.

> By-and-by, when he is old enough, take the child into confidence;
> let him know what a noble thing it is to be able to make himself
> do, in a minute, and brightly, the very thing he would rather not
> do. (*Home Education*, p. 164)

And when children's small wills are exhausted, a parent can
provide a distraction for them. Small children aren't fully ready to
take on this responsibility for themselves. Eight- or ten-year-old
children are perfectly able to comprehend this concept, but even then
it will be some time before they are able to command themselves fully
and distract themselves by changing their own thoughts. A parent's
assistance to support a child's will gives him a chance to do as much
as he can on his own, and if you can provide a distraction when one
is needed, he will be just a little stronger next time.

A Person Should Exercise Will

Exercising your will is part of what it means to be a person and
to develop the self-knowledge that a person ought to have. It is your
will that makes you a mature person who is able to act virtuously. You
do not have to be a slave to your wants. The seventeenth principle
begins, "Children should be taught, to distinguish between 'I want'
and 'I will'" (*Philosophy of Education*, p. xxxi).

I want is governed by every natural appetite or desire we have—and
our human nature is made up of many. We desire ease and pleasure,
approbation and reward, and all those wants have their place. They
are good servants but bad masters. There is an order in the world,
and the better we understand that order and authority and suppress
our "wants" when we should so that we act in harmony with that
authority, the better persons we will be. We must *will* those acts and
choices, and then when our wills are exhausted we must learn how to
rest our wills to refresh them for continued service.

Our personhood places us in a universe that is governed by order
and authority. We are always going to be serving something, and if
that something is only ourselves, we become the servants—even the
slaves—of our own desires and appetites, which can lead us into deep

pits of addiction and despair. When we choose to serve something outside ourselves because we have learned to love that idea or person more than ourselves, we are using our wills—we are acting like persons. In all things, small or great, the vital work of the world is done by persons who exercise *will*.

A Person Possesses Reason

Reason Provides Logical Demonstration

This "way of the will" is followed by the eighteenth principle in which Miss Mason addressed "the way of reason:"

> We teach children, too, not to "lean (too confidently) to their own understanding"; because the function of reason is to give logical demonstration. (*Philosophy of Education*, p. xxxi)

The ability to give a logical demonstration is useful in some areas, but is not altogether reliable, as we shall see. All the principles operate in relation to each other, which is consistent with the idea that a *science of relations*—an essential harmony—is present at all times. Apart from their place in the principles as a whole, these two principles concerning will and reason have a special relationship with each other.

As with the will, reason is the second thing that sets a person apart from all other creatures. Animals cannot reason, cannot follow a logical argument, cannot ascertain truths that reason alone—such as the laws of physics or grammar—can perceive.

However, the first thing Miss Mason wanted us to know is that reason is not infallible and can be dangerous. She warned that "he who reasons without knowledge is like a child playing with edged tools" (*Philosophy of Education*, p. 315). Of course, sharp-edged tools are extremely useful. The meals you will eat today, the clothes you are wearing, the bed you slept in, and the building you're sitting in were all provided with the use of sharp-edged tools. The world wouldn't function well without such tools. However, they are dangerous when handled improperly, and that's what she wants us to understand.

Reason functions to give us logical demonstration. In the realm of pure logic—for example, mathematics—it works very well. It's an obvious fact that 2 + 2 = 4, and when we understand the rationale of addition, similar problems such as 17 + 30 are very quickly resolved, and our reason assures us that the answer is correct. There's no room for dispute or variations of opinion. But reason also functions to provide us with logical demonstration of an initial *idea* that has been accepted, and this is where we must exercise care and employ our wills.

We know that *children are born persons,* and one aspect of personhood is a mind that feeds and grows on ideas. However, not every idea is healthy and correct. If you were the ruler of a small kingdom and wanted to be the ruler of a larger one, the idea of invading a neighboring country might arise, for example. If your neighbor had an apple orchard, the idea of collecting his ripe apples after dark one evening might occur to you. Ideas are many and of various kinds.

Reason Functions without a Moral Compass

According to Miss Mason, if we *choose*—with the will—to entertain an idea, our reason goes to work. In the same way that our reason cannot help but lead us to the correct answer to 17 + 30, it goes to work on the ideas we accept and brings them to logical conclusions or provides logical demonstration of their correctness. She reminded her readers that Shakespeare's Macbeth accepted the idea that he was destined to be king, and the logical conclusion of that idea led to the murder of the existing king. It was perfectly *reasonable,* but it was not *right,* and that is what makes reason a sharp-edged tool. Like a honed blade, it is effective but has no moral compass of its own. Relying on reason may lead us into grave error:

> Perhaps every failure in conduct, in individuals, and in nations, is due to the confusion which exists as to that which is logically right, as established by the reason, and that which is morally right, as established by external law. (*Parents and Children,* p. 241)

Miss Mason assured us, "There is no notion a man chooses to receive which his reason will not justify" (*Philosophy of Education,* p. 55). If you accept the idea that you should invade a neighboring country, reason will provide plenty of good, logical proofs to support that idea. Your people need more land. You have better agricultural techniques that will improve their farming. Their leader is a bad one. There will be plenty of *reasonable* support for your plan to invade or even to appropriate your neighbor's apples if you entertain that idea. Reason is never at a loss to supply a logical argument, but as we have seen, we live in an ordered universe with a moral authority that it is our responsibility to obey.

> We, personally, might or might not be trusted to come to a morally right conclusion from any premise we entertain. But the reasoning power, acting in a more or less mechanical and involuntary manner, does not necessarily work towards the morally right conclusion. All that reason does for us is to prove, logically, any idea we choose to entertain....How necessary then that a child should be instructed to understand the limitations of his own reason, so that he will not confound logical demonstration with eternal truth. (*School Education*, p. 116)

It is easy to suppose that a logical conclusion must be true, but that is exactly what Miss Mason wanted us *not* to do. Because our reason works in this way—charging forward to find logical demonstration for ideas that we have accepted—we must turn our attention to those ideas. We have to guard our thoughts and take care not to allow wrong ideas to get their foothold. This is an important aspect of knowing ourselves and governing ourselves as we ought to do. We need to know how the human psyche works. If we know that our reason is going to support an idea we accept, we have an obligation to keep an idea at arm's length and make a choice with our wills about whether or not we are going to give it room in our thoughts. Throughout history many people have been deceived into believing that they can trust their reason—that reason is really the only authority anyone has. Miss Mason lamented:

> Many thoughtful and good people believe that there is no higher authority; that to act according to his own Reason is the best that can be expected of any man. (*Ourselves*, Book I, p. 61)

When it comes to reason, we can trust it to steer us straight about math—two and two always equal four. However, in other matters, reasonable conclusions can be right or wrong. The validity of reasonable conclusions depends on the truth or rightness of the initial idea.

We have a responsibility to check our ideas at the doors of our minds before letting them in.

Miss Mason told us that two people can be convinced by reason of two absolutely opposing positions. We see this all the time.

> On questions of war and peace and politics, of religion, of education, of public works, of clothing, of food, in fact, upon any and every point, you will find it possible that the Reason of equally good and equally intelligent people will bring them to quite opposite conclusions. That is the cause of all the controversy in the world. People think that they can convince each other by the arguments which their own Reason has accepted. So they could, if the other side were not already convinced by arguments exactly opposite; and upon which side a man is convinced, usually depends upon his own will. (*Ourselves*, Book I, p. 61)

Reason Must Be Subordinate to Knowledge of Truth

If the initial idea that we choose to accept is not right and true, our flawless reason and logic will lead us to a conclusion that must also be false. Reason is not an infallible guide, and this is where the danger lies. We cannot trust reason to give us truth. Rather, we have to evaluate the truth of our premises—those initial ideas. We have to compare them to some kind of external, absolute standards that we can apply. Because we are persons, we have the gift of reason—a useful, sharp-edged tool. But what do we need in order to wield it well? Miss Mason said:

> It is a fatal error to think that reason can take the place of knowledge, that reason is infallible, that reasonable conclusions are of necessity right conclusions. Reason is a man's servant, not his master; and behaves like a good and faithful servant...and brings logical demonstration of any premise which the will chooses to entertain. But the will is the man, the will chooses; and the man must *know*, if the will is to make just and discriminating decisions. (*Philosophy of Education*, p. 314)

If we are born persons who have a responsibility to understand what it means to be a person—"Know thyself"—then we have to learn this about ourselves. Our reason is not an infallible guide, so we need knowledge of Truth in order to safeguard our choices. That opens another line of inquiry: How do we know whether or not an idea is true and one we should accept? The answer is embedded in the nineteenth principle:

> Children should be taught, as they become mature enough to understand such teaching, that the chief responsibility which rests on them as *persons* is the acceptance or rejection of ideas. *To help them in this choice we give them principles of conduct, and a wide range of the knowledge fitted to them.* (*Philosophy of Education*, p. xxx, emphasis added)

All of the things that are included in the curriculum of a Charlotte Mason education supply this need for knowledge. We read history and literature and poetry to give us some background for understanding the ways of men, the passions that drive them, and the consequences of various courses of action. We read the Bible to understand divine law and how it shapes our perspective of the way that the world works. We polish our use of language so that we can communicate our thoughts well, and we hone our reason in mathematical disciplines. Bit by bit—line upon line, precept upon precept—we develop educated consciences, which we hope will be underpinned by character that is strong enough to make right choices when ideas are presented to us.

Miss Mason described the way this might work:

> His knowledge affords him a standard by which he judges the worth of such opinion; his principles, a test of its moral rightness. Therefore the flashy new opinion, which history tells him has been tried and found wanting long ago, has no chance with him. He examines it in the light of his principles, finds it to be based on an error of thought, that it leads to further errors of thought and action; and it takes no hold upon his mind. (*Ourselves*, Book II, p. 62)

As educators, we hope to help our students use their reason without becoming overly confident in it. Thoughts and ideas accost us all the time, but we have a will—we can make choices. We don't have to let every idea take possession of our minds. The wider and deeper our knowledge of truth is, the easier it will be to determine whether or not an idea is true. When we have accepted or rejected an idea, reason will step in to confirm things for us. We will soon have a multitude of irresistible proofs to back up the idea we have accepted—proofs that will protect us from being swayed by different opinions.

However, in order to have the resources to know what is right to choose, we must have a wide and generous education. We must have knowledge, and that will grow gradually as we read and think and observe and learn. Because all knowledge has its source in God, all knowledge will increase our understanding of the world and the way His truth manifests itself. As persons, we each have a conscience that makes us want to do right, but we are not born knowing what exactly is right and wrong. Everything we learn is part of what educates our consciences, and educated consciences will be able to guide us in making choices in a way that reason can never do.

Part II

Not Without Hope

There is no education but self-education and only as the young student works with his own mind is anything effected. But we are not without hope.

—Charlotte Mason, *A Philosophy of Education*

9

How Shall We Then Teach

The teacher is no longer the mere instrument
of forcible intellectual feeding.
—Charlotte Mason, *A Philosophy of Education*

Instruments for Educating a Person

Teaching Methods Must Be Consistent with the Principles

Now that we have examined the "few broad principles" that cover the field of education, it is time to consider how this is supposed to work itself out practically. We understand that children are born persons whose characters must be nurtured and that they live in an ordered world with which they must form many vital relationships because they have hungry minds that require proper food to grow.

But we must still address one of the large questions of education: How are we going to teach? What methods will we use? Once we accept the basic propositions that education is about forming character and building relationships, we still want to know what that looks like during school time for a six-year-old, a ten-year-old, or a sixteen-year-old. We have to fill the school hours with something. What are we actually going to do?

I have reserved several principles until this point in our discussion. We have covered the principles that provide a philosophical framework for education, and we will now consider the methods that we will use to implement those principles. If we try to simply pick up the suggestions Charlotte Mason made for *how* to conduct education without appreciating their relationship to the central principles, we run the risk of allowing the methods to degenerate into a mechanical system.

Because *children are born persons* and *education is the science of relations*, the task of education is to acquaint a child with what it means to be a person who has reason and will and who lives in a world of order and authority in which he has duties and obligations to fulfill. He must learn to use his own will to choose what is right *because* it is right and then to rely on his reason to support him in the choices he makes.

Our Teaching Must Educate a Child's Conscience

But how will he know what the right choices are? This is where the more practical aspects of education must begin. We are feeding the minds of our children with a view toward educating their consciences. Because they are persons, they are aware that there is a moral authority in the world—an *ought* that implies duties they owe to God and man. However, although they are born with that sense of *ought*, they do not innately know what those duties are. They have the possibility to be virtuous but also to be evil. Before they will be able to make right choices, they have to learn what is right and what is wrong.

Having established that we cannot use artificial means to motivate children, what are we left with? In the fifth principle, Miss Mason laid out the tools we are free to use:

> We are limited to three educational instruments—the atmosphere of environment, the discipline of habit, and the presentation of living ideas. (*Philosophy of Education*, p. xxix)

We are limited to these three instruments because of the fourth educational principle, which prohibits educators from encroaching on the personhood of children. However, Miss Mason wanted us to be encouraged by what is possible, not discouraged because some things are off-limits.

> Having cut out the direct use of fear or love, suggestion or influence, undue play upon any one natural desire, emulation, for

example, we are no longer free to use all means in the education of children. There are but three left for our use and to each of these we must give careful study or we shall not realise how great a scope is left to us. (*Philosophy of Education*, p. 94)

I've saved this part of the discussion until now because I think these three instruments will be better understood in light of the fuller discussion we've had about personhood and relationships. Miss Mason's principles can be applied both by parents in the home and by teachers in a school setting. We are free to use atmosphere, discipline, and life to educate children in either of those situations.

Education Is an Atmosphere

Natural Conditions Create Atmosphere

The first instrument is the "atmosphere of environment." In the sixth principle, Miss Mason was careful to assure us that she did not mean that the child's environment should be carefully constructed in some special way to accommodate him. Rather, she wanted us to understand how the circumstances of his life form a part of a child's education in a natural way. What this means is that rather than creating a perfect, sheltered environment for our children, like plants in a hothouse, we allow them to grow up with natural exposure to life as it is.

For parents, it is a good idea to recognize that we do not have complete control over these conditions. Think about atmosphere in its literal meaning—the air we breathe. Of course, it has the oxygen we need—we can't live without it. But it is also full of foreign particles and things that aren't needed or even healthy. Although we cannot fully control a child's atmosphere, exposure to hard things does not always produce negative results. We cannot protect our children from everything, and we must remember that we are not alone in the work of educating them.

> Here is a matter which sometimes causes uneasiness to parents: they are appalled when they think of the casual circumstances and chance people that may have a lasting effect upon their children's characters. But their part is, perhaps, to exercise ordinary

prudence and not over-much direction. They have no means of knowing what will reach a child; whether the evil which blows his way may not incline him to good, or whether the too-insistent . good may not predispose him to evil. Perhaps the forces of life as they come should be allowed to play upon the child, who is not, be it remembered, a product of educational care, but a person whose spiritual nurture is accomplished by that wind which bloweth whither it listeth. (*Formation of Character*, p. 277)

The atmosphere that is one-third of our educational tools is primarily made up of "the forces of life as they come." It is important that it all be genuine. Miss Mason warned against an artificial environment. Children have real duties and real virtues to implement. They play a role in the happiness or unhappiness of the people around them. The order and tidiness of the home are within their grasp. The hours define their days as they do for adults. The daily routine of the home creates the atmosphere in which children live, and that atmosphere is part of what educates them.

It is not an environment that [children] want, a set of artificial relations carefully constructed, but an *atmosphere* which nobody has been at pains to constitute. It is there, about the child, his natural element, precisely as the atmosphere of the earth is about us. It is thrown off, as it were, from persons and things, stirred by events, sweetened by love, ventilated, kept in motion, by the regulated action of common sense. (*Philosophy of Education*, p. 96)

We Also Contribute to the Atmosphere

The things that you value and make time for in your everyday life will teach your children what is important. In other words, you are helping them to order their loves and form their affections. They are learning something by the choices you make about how you use your time, spend your money, and interact with the people around you.

But atmosphere is not just the physical environment. There is also an atmosphere of ideas. Do we bow our heads to pray? Are we reading new books and talking about what we are learning? Do we make plans to visit elderly relatives as often as possible or make a meal to take to someone who needs one? Are we talking about current events, planning ways to serve and give, noticing that tasks that need to be done and taking initiative to do something about them? No family is perfect, but the things that matter to us add to the atmosphere that is educating our children.

Although home atmosphere probably has the stronger influence on a child, a school can also create an atmosphere that forms a part of a child's education. Miss Mason described what it could be:

> The bracing atmosphere of truth and sincerity should be perceived in every School; and here again the common pursuit of knowledge by teacher and class comes to our aid and creates a Current of fresh air perceptible even to the chance visitor, who sees the glow of intellectual life and moral health on the faces of teachers and children alike. (*Philosophy of Education*, p. 97)

The circumstances in which a child lives or shares community with others help to shape his character. Kevin Clark and Ravi Jain, the authors of *The Liberal Arts Tradition*, explain that in a school, "The culture is as much a teacher as the curriculum" (p. 108). The culture of home, school, even church or neighborhood plays a role in the education of a child.

Because we cannot and should not aim to create a perfect atmosphere, we should not allow this educational instrument to discourage us. Just as there are warm days and cold days in our natural environment, there are good days and bad days in our home environment. Atmosphere is an instrument of education, not a wall of protection. Sometimes we learn important lessons when conditions are uncomfortable. Miss Mason reminded us:

> Is it not the shocks of adversity and not cotton wool protection that evolve true manhood? (*Philosophy of Education*, p. 96)

Miss Mason considered this atmosphere to be fully one-third of a child's education, so even though we cannot control it entirely, it will repay our efforts to give it some thought. At the very least, this atmosphere will be most effective if it is in harmony with the direct teaching we choose to give. The arbitrary "do as I say, not as I do" does not work at all—we feel the injustice of it, and so do the children. You cannot say, "Take off your muddy shoes when you come in the door" if you do not do likewise. You cannot say, "Pick up your things and put them away when you are done" if you leave your own projects spread across the table. Consistency is the problem we struggle with on a daily basis. If the children see us at least trying, even if we sometimes fail, that will be a part of the atmosphere, too—we try. There are cloudy days as well as sunny days, and part of the atmosphere in our home is our response to failures. Sometimes there are natural consequences, but there is also the grace of forgiveness and forbearance.

Since we cannot fully control atmosphere, it may be that the best thing we can do is simply remember that it is part of our educational toolbox and be aware of its influence. If it grows stale, we can open a window to freshen things up—change our routines. We can perfume the air with a spritz of something novel and surprising now and then. The carefree work of atmosphere leaves us more attention for the other tools at our disposal.

Education Is a Discipline

Habits Develop Naturally

The goal of education is the formation of character—instilling virtue in our children. A virtuous person is one who knows what is right, desires to do right, and makes the choices that result in right actions. As we have seen, the will is the man. However, making choices exhausts the will. An important method of easing that task is the formation of habits. Many good actions can be made a matter of habit that will not require the constant effort of choice. Many virtues— such as courtesy, truthfulness, and obedience—can become ingrained habits.

Charlotte Mason told us in the seventh principle that we must purposefully instill good habits like these because they will lay a foundation for what will become the character of a person. She quoted a bit of well-known wisdom that is attributed to Aristotle:

> As has been well said, "Sow an act, reap a habit; sow a habit, reap a character; sow a character, reap a destiny." And a great function of the educator is to secure that acts shall be so regularly, purposefully, and methodically sown that the child shall reap the

habits of the good life, in thinking and doing, with the minimum of conscious effort. (*Parents and Children*, p. 124)

This is why the second instrument of education that we are free to use with persons who are forming relationships is "the discipline of habit." We are creatures of habit, and as Miss Mason told us, habit is *inevitable*. The habits may be good or bad, but it is our nature to fall into habitual ways because habits are the smooth rails upon which life can run, saving us from having to make decisions about everything from what to eat for breakfast to which route to drive to work.

> Habit is inevitable. If we fail to ease life by laying down habits of right thinking and right acting, habits of wrong thinking and wrong acting fix themselves of their own accord....Habit is like fire, a bad master but an indispensable servant; and probably one reason for the nervous scrupulosity, hesitation, indecision of our day, is that life was not duly eased for us in the first place by those whose business it was to lay down lines of habit upon which our behaviour might run easily. (*Philosophy of Education*, p. 101)

Good Habits Take Effort to Develop

Miss Mason called this instrument a discipline because it does take discipline to ensure that it is good habits and not bad ones that are formed. If you want to develop good habits in your children (and in yourself), you will have to do the disciplinary work of watching over the process until the habit is established. I have seen a small child of three enter a house and immediately remove her shoes, placing them where they belong. There was no difficulty, and it took only a moment, but it represented the discipline of a parent who reminded the child and removed the shoes herself if necessary many, many times. But the parent who invested in that discipline can look forward to another ten years of tidily put-away shoes, and that makes the discipline worth the effort.

There are three keys to habit formation that should help us succeed in the process. First, a habit should be grounded in an inspiring idea. If a child has been encouraged to appreciate orderliness, putting away the shoes serves a higher purpose than simply doing something for an arbitrary reason. Second, only one new habit should be addressed at a time. Because of the effort involved in establishing a habit, it is wise not to dilute that effort by doing too many new things at once. Last, perfect consistency—that effort of discipline—must be maintained until the habit is thoroughly formed. If you have very young children—age six and under—you can probably work on one habit at a time yourself without their awareness, but older children need to know what habit you are working on and why. Their intelligent cooperation will make the process much easier, but good habits cannot be instilled without the investment of time and discipline.

> It is unnecessary to enumerate those habits which we should aim at forming, for everyone knows more about these than anyone practises. We admire the easy carriage of the soldier but shrink from the discipline which is able to produce it. We admire the lady who can sit upright through a long dinner, who in her old age prefers a straight chair because she has arrived at due muscular balance and has done so by a course of discipline. There is no other way of forming any good habit, though the discipline is usually that of the internal government which the person exercises upon himself; but a certain strenuousness in the formation of good habits is necessary because every such habit is the result of conflict. The bad habit of the easy life is always pleasant and persuasive and to be resisted with pain and effort, but with hope and certainty of success, because in our very structure is the preparation for forming such habits of muscle and mind as we deliberately propose to ourselves. (*Philosophy of Education*, pp. 101–2)

A great deal of right thinking and acting can be established as a matter of habit if we make the effort and are consistent. In some of her earlier writing, Miss Mason was especially enthusiastic about the latest scientific ideas which suggested that habits created physical changes in the brain. Whatever a child's "nature"—those good or bad tendencies he was born with—creating a habit supposedly rewired the brain to act differently. This was the logic behind her claim that "habit is ten natures" (*Home Education*, p. 96). The nurturing of a deliberate habit should have a stronger influence on a child than even his inborn tendencies. Later in her life, she was somewhat disappointed that the science was not quite as definitive as she had hoped, but the role of habit in education has a long tradition that is not dependent on how well we understand the mechanism of it. The fact that good habits lay a foundation for good character is well established.

Habits Support Our Other Educational Endeavors

Cultivating good habits is an important one-third of our educational instruments. We are developing a child's conscience and teaching him to use his will, but good habits make the path a little smoother until maturity is reached and the child is able to fully command his own actions.

> The training of the will, the instruction of the conscience, and, so far as it lies with us, the development of the divine life in the child, are carried on simultaneously with this training in the habits of a good life; and these last will carry the child safely over the season of infirm will, immature conscience, until he is able to take, under direction from above, the conduct of his life, the moulding of his character, into his own hands. (*Parents and Children*, p. 91)

Miss Mason encouraged parents to be diligent in this discipline of forming habits for their children. If a child had a particular fault, she urged parents to address the fault by instilling the opposite good habit and by simply making no room in the child's life for the exercise of the fault until the new habit was established. The discipline of focusing on one habit at a time can be a powerful educational tool in the hands of a thoughtful parent.

While many of the habits we want to instill in our children are for the sake of their character, there are also intellectual habits that will make learning easier. One of the key habits that will aid education is the habit of attention. A person who is able to bring his full attention to something will apprehend it more quickly and remember it better than a person whose mind is wandering and not fully engaged by the material at hand.

Just as habits of living make our lives run more smoothly because they free us from the effort of decision, mental habits can be established that will similarly make the work of the student easier. As we will see in the next chapter, Miss Mason's school practices were founded upon the concept of developing sound intellectual habits.

But good habits—physical, intellectual, and moral—can be achieved in one way only, and that is through the application of discipline. The hope of making life and education a little easier by the formation of good habits should be the incentive we need to invest in the effort of discipline.

Education Is a Life

A Child's Hungry Mind Needs to Be Nourished Well

That brings us to the eighth principle and the final instrument of education permitted to us. This one, too, is based upon the two key principles—children are born persons who have minds that hunger for knowledge, and education must encourage them to form relationships. Based upon these ideas, the third instrument is "education is a life," which means that just as a living body requires sustenance, so does the living mind. The proper food for the mind is *ideas,* as we discussed in chapter 7. Our bodies need to be fed, and so do our minds.

This analogy is far-reaching; almost every principle that governs the wise choice of food for the body has a corollary principle in the choice of intellectual food for the mind. The healthiest nourishment is unadulterated and natural, and children should be served knowledge that has not been predigested or overly processed. Children need generous quantities of food served at regular intervals to feed their bodies, and their minds also need frequent exposure to fresh ideas. Just as there are cheap, unhealthy substitutes for real food, so there are light and fluffy books that do not satisfy their intellectual needs. They must eat a balanced diet of various foods to maintain physical health, and their minds also hunger to know many different things. They must be offered a wide range of knowledge, as we have seen— knowledge of God and man and the universe.

We do not have to teach children to swallow and digest. They are fully equipped to eat and absorb their proper food, and if the food is adequate, we can rely on natural processes to produce results. Children grow physically when they are properly fed. If the principle that children are born persons with capable minds is true, it means that they are also naturally equipped to deal with knowledge, and they will grow intellectually if they are properly fed. Just as with the food we offer, children will take and reject according to their own needs:

> Probably he will reject nine-tenths of the ideas we offer, as he makes use of only a small proportion of his bodily food, rejecting the rest. He is an eclectic; he may choose this or that; our business is to supply him with due abundance and variety and his to take what he needs. Urgency on our part annoys him. He resists forcible feeding and loathes predigested food. What suits him best is pabulum presented in the indirect literary form which Our Lord adopts in those wonderful parables....One other caution; it seems to be necessary to present ideas with a great deal of padding, as they reach us in a novel or poem or history book written with literary power. (*Philosophy of Education*, p. 109)

Once all of these things are taken into consideration, Miss Mason's final conclusion is that children should read books. The mind takes in ideas best when they are clothed in literary language, taking the form of a story or a narrative, and therefore:

> The only vital method of education appears to be that children should read worthy books, many worthy books. (*Philosophy of Education*, p. 12)

Nourishing Ideas Will Bear Fruit in a Child's Character

If you consider the full scope of Miss Mason's educational philosophy, the exact role of this principle will become clearer. We know that *children are born persons* and that *education is the science of relations*. We know that these two primary principles overlap to show us our need of knowing ourselves, particularly our very human functions of will and reason. We know that our reason will justify the ideas our will has accepted, but we need our education to give us the knowledge that will guide us to *know* what is right so that we can choose wisely.

With all of that in mind, "education is a life which must be sustained upon ideas" makes sense. A child will take in an idea—the idea of honor, of loyalty, of generosity, of patience. The idea is a living seed that will germinate in his mind, take root, and grow. It will bear fruit when he uses his will to choose an action in harmony with the idea he has taken in. He may choose to come clean about a fault he has committed rather than sneak and lie. He might stand up for his sister when she is being teased by other children. He may put his own money into an offering taken up for a missionary in a foreign country. He might determine to continue being kind to the neighbor who scowls at him in hopes that she will eventually relent and be friendly. Children have it in them to show greatness of heart and soul. They can only bring those possibilities to fruition when they are nourished with great ideas.

But the educator—even a parent—cannot know exactly which ideas a child needs, which ones will call forth virtuous responses. That's why Miss Mason called upon us to sow the seed, not to stint, and to provide children with a generous curriculum—a course of wide reading that encompasses all the areas of knowledge. *Education is the science of relations*, and a child needs a chance to form relationships in every direction with the hungry octopus of his mind. We cannot distill an idea and present it to him in a clinical way and expect it to have the same effect. The ideas that reach a child's heart are conveyed there by books and stories that arrest his attention, hold his interest, and inspire him to care.

> A child cannot in mind or body live upon tabloids [artificial vitamin tablets] however scientifically prepared; out of a whole big book he may not get more than half a dozen of those ideas upon which his spirit thrives; and they come in unexpected places and unrecognised forms, so that no grown person is capable of making such extracts from Scott or Dickens or Milton, as will certainly give him nourishment. It is a case of, — "In the morning sow thy seed and in the evening withhold not thine hand for thou knowest not whether shall prosper, either this or that." (*Philosophy of Education*, pp. 109–10)

History, literature, and poetry, as well as books about nature and travel, are all fodder for a child's mind. These are taken in and become the storehouse from which a child will draw when he is presented with an idea that requires a conscious choice. The nineteenth principle states "to help them in this choice we give them principles of conduct, and a wide range of the knowledge fitted to them" (*Philosophy of Education*, p. xxxi). We do that by providing them with a steady diet of books on a wide variety of subjects.

A Child Grows Only from the Nourishment He Digests for Himself

Children will not absorb every possible principle from every book that they read. Nevertheless, if the seed is sown, they will find what they need. One reason the books are so critical is that they provide "a great deal of padding" (*Philosophy of Education*, p. 109), which Miss Mason said is necessary to their assimilation. Bald, didactic statements such as "Honesty is the best policy" will not touch the heart and mind of a child in the same way as a story in which honesty—or dishonesty—is presented in the form of a hero who acts out the little drama that illustrates the law at hand, provided the book does not fall to moralizing for the child. Miss Mason urged us to let each child draw the moral for himself. True education requires the work of the individual, and it is only the ideas that a person perceives and accepts for himself that have an effect on his character. No one can eat and digest food for someone else. This is what she means when she says there is no education but self-education:

> There is no education but self-education, and as soon as a young child begins his education he does so as a student. Our business is to give him mind-stuff, and both quality and quantity are essential. Naturally, each of us possesses this mind-stuff only in limited measure, but we know where to procure it; for the best thought the world possesses is stored in books; we must open books to children, the best books; our own concern is abundant provision and orderly serving. (*Philosophy of Education*, p. 26)

What a child does not take in and digest for himself is no more a part of him than the clothing he puts on in the morning and tosses into a corner at night (unless he has developed the much better habit of putting them into a hamper)—adornment for the moment, but not a lasting part of the person himself. As educators, we want to give our students more than temporary adornments, however impressive they might appear for the moment. True education will have an impact on the child's heart and mind. He will be a different person—a better person—with each idea he takes in and makes his own, and the best way to ensure that he gets what he needs is to offer a generous feast—a wide curriculum of every kind of idea. Miss Mason reminded us that this principle is part of understanding that a child is a person:

A person is not built up from without but within, that is, he is *living*, and all external educational appliances and activities which are intended to mould his character are decorative and not vital.

This sounds like a stale truism; but, let us consider a few corollaries of the notion that "a child is a person," and that a person is, primarily, living. Now no external application is capable of nourishing life or promoting growth; baths of wine, wrappings of velvet have no effect upon physical life except as they may hinder it; life is sustained on that which is taken in by the organism, not by that which is applied from without. (*Philosophy of Education*, pp. 23–24)

These three instruments of education—atmosphere, discipline, living ideas—are the tools we can use to educate a person toward virtue. This is not an education whose object is passing exams, getting good grades, and being accepted at a prestigious school, although children may well get those things by the way. This is an educational paradigm that aims much higher—toward giving a child every chance to become the best possible person he can be. Yes, children are born persons with active minds, but they are not born fully developed persons who think rightly and bring those thoughts to bear on their actions by choosing to do what is right over and over again. That is our work, and we are not without hope that it can be accomplished.

10

Bathing in the Jordan

> Education is slack and uncertain for the lack
> of sound principles exactly applied.
> —Charlotte Mason, *A Philosophy of Education*

Principles Must Be Supported by Good Practices

Charlotte Mason articulated all the principles we have covered so far in the synopsis of her philosophy that was shared with the PNEU in 1904 and included at the beginning of all her volumes in 1905 (*The Story of Charlotte Mason*, pp. 109–10). This is a comprehensive and complete picture of what education should be, with a strong indication of how it might be accomplished. It is a unifying philosophy, but not a complete pedagogy. It is, however, the foundation of any robust pedagogy that can embrace these principles and apply them. We have a powerful foundation in the primary principles that *children are born persons* and *education is the science of relations*, but the question still arises: How will those relations be formed?

> We have relations with what there is in the present and with what there has been in the past, with what is above us, and about us; and that fulness of living and serviceableness depend for each of us upon how far we apprehend these relationships and how many of them we lay hold of. Every child is heir to an enormous patrimony. The question is, what are the formalities necessary to put him in possession of that which is his? (*School Education*, p. 218)

As with many things, sometimes the most effective methods seem a little *too* simple. Miss Mason was well aware of the tendency to take a dim view of something that seems a bit pedestrian. In her final book, *A Philosophy of Education*, published posthumously in 1925, she wanted to present her educational philosophy and its working methods to the British public at large, and she wrote:

> My object in offering this volume to the public is to urge upon all who are concerned with education a few salient principles which are generally either unknown or disregarded; and a few methods which, like that bathing in Jordan [Elijah's requirement for the leper Naaman in II Kings 5], are too simple to commend themselves to the "general." Yet these principles and methods make education entirely effectual. (*Philosophy of Education*, pp. xxvi–xxvii)

We have already discussed the "few salient principles" at length, and we are now ready to consider practical methods. After Miss Mason developed a school and a curriculum founded on these principles, she came to believe that certain practices were vital to working them out. Therefore, when that final book was published in 1925, it included an additional three practical principles that had been added "for the use of teachers" (Cholmondeley, *The Story of Charlotte Mason*, p. 295). The philosophical principles apply to education both in the realm of bringing up children and in academics. These practical principles are intended to govern the academic application of the philosophy. She was a little concerned that her simple methods might not appeal to modern educators, and like Naaman's servant, she urged them—and us—to give them a fair trial.

A Child Needs a Broad Curriculum of Excellent Books

The thirteenth principle tells us that in "devising a syllabus [curriculum] for a normal child" (*Philosophy of Education*, p. xxx), three considerations must be adhered to. The knowledge presented must be generous, varied, and literary. These requirements are based on principles that we have already discussed at length, with the two primary principles—*children are born persons* and *education is the science of relations*—encompassing all the rest.

With this understanding in mind, a child's curriculum must meet his need for adequate sustenance, for we are educating a hungry, growing mind. We cannot offer knowledge by grudging teaspoonfuls. The dishes must be heaped up with plenty so that the child can help himself to as much as he is hungry for. But the dishes on the table must also be various—of many different kinds. We have already discussed this, but the science of relations demands that the child have the opportunity to develop a taste for all kinds of knowledge. Thus, the curriculum offered to a student in a Charlotte Mason paradigm is wide.

This serves two purposes in the end. The first, of course, is that the child does form relations with all the various kinds of knowledge. The second is that the child has enough exposure to various things, so that he can begin to see the outlines of their relations to each other—not unlike the early stages of putting a puzzle together, where like parts are grouped with like and a straight-edged frame begins to emerge. The ordered universe—the cosmos—in which a person lives is whole and harmonious, and everything from language to math to nature study echoes and resounds the same profound truths.

Miss Mason referred to "a great educational principle which was better understood by the medieval Church than by ourselves" (*School Education*, p. 153), which she called "the Great Recognition." It was just what we have discussed in chapter 3—that all knowledge is connected by its common source. All knowledge comes to us from God.

This perception of unified knowledge in the world has a long tradition:

> The entire medieval vision of reality was conceived from the perspective of an ordered unity—a cosmos comprised of both whole and parts. While the ancient Pre-Socratics and Pythagoreans developed the concept of an ordered cosmos, the medievals understood it as creation ordered by Christ, the *logos*, under the creative impulse of God. (Clark and Jain, *The Liberal Arts Tradition*, p. 97)

When we lack this unified understanding of the cosmos, our studies feel disconnected, and many educational philosophies address this problem by reducing the number of things studied. However, when we understand that education is the science of relations, we do not want to curtail those relations. Miss Mason believed that a variety of subjects kept a student's interest fresh, and her view was shared by the ancient educator Quintilian:

> Why should we not divide our hours of study among a number of different subjects? Especially as change of occupation in itself refreshes and restores the mind. (*Quintilian on Education*, p. 65)

The Excellent Books Must Be Narrated

Apart from the consideration that the knowledge must be generous and varied, Miss Mason made a principle of the fact that children must be educated with literary books from the very beginning. Because of this principle, any curriculum based on this philosophy will look like a fairly long book list, with the books falling under a variety of headings—science, history, literature, biography, geography—and an examination of those books should reveal that every one of them is an example of fine, literary language.

But the book list is just a starting point, and we cannot carry out the principles with even an excellent list of books. The child must be placed in the right relationship with the books he reads. Miss Mason had seen a mere book list fall short:

> I feel strongly that to attempt to work this method without a firm adherence to the few principles laid down would be not only idle but disastrous. "Oh, we could do anything with books like those," said a master; he tried the books and failed conspicuously because he ignored the principles. (*Philosophy of Education*, p. 270)

This principle of a generous curriculum of living books must be accompanied with the correct use of them, and the next few practices that Miss Mason established as principles show us the very simple way that she had found effectual.

The fourteenth principle explains:

> As knowledge is not assimilated until it is reproduced, children should "tell back" after a single reading or hearing: or should write on some part of what they have read. (*Philosophy of Education*, p. xxx)

This is, of course, narration. I have written extensively elsewhere about narration, which is a method I believe in very strongly. However, I will include a brief discussion here as no consideration of Miss Mason's principles could be complete without devoting some thought to this. Reading excellent books and narrating from them are the primary work of school education.

> [Children] should read to know...[and] their knowledge should be tested, not by questions, but by the oral (and occasionally the written) reproduction of a passage after one reading; all further processes that we concern ourselves about in teaching, the mind performs for itself; and, lastly, this sort of reading should be the chief business in the class room. (*Philosophy of Education*, pp. 341-42)

Narration Develops Excellent Thinking Skills

As I have said repeatedly, *education is the science of relations*, and the reason narration is so foundational as a practice is that it is a *relationship-building* method. Narration is just as simple as "telling back" sounds in practice, but it contains the seeds of so much more.

For younger children, a parent or teacher reads the material of a lesson, and the child tells back what has been read in his own words. This practice is immediately going to develop that mental habit of attention, which we discussed earlier, because the only way to narrate well is to pay attention. You might have to begin by reading only a paragraph or two before asking for narration, but over time—and you can take several years to do this—a child will grow into the ability to narrate a whole chapter at a time.

There is an element of original composition in narration. The child does not parrot back the sentences of the reading, but restates things in his own way. This action of his own mind on the material at hand is composition, and early oral narration lays a foundation for later written work.

The act of narration builds vocabulary as children begin to incorporate the words in their books into their own narrations. It also builds an intuitive sense of grammar and language based upon real understanding. Narration assists memory because the mental act of going over the material in the mind and restating it in words and sentences is a kind of digestion of that feast that has been laid, and what we digest becomes a part of us.

Although telling back is simple on the surface, a great deal of high-level thinking goes into producing even a basic narration. A narration must begin and continue in some kind of order, and ordering the material—chronologically or otherwise—is a higher-level thinking skill. The child must also evaluate the relative importance of what he has heard and select material for his narration. Which are the most important things to include? What incidental details will be set aside? The process is largely natural and unconscious, but it is happening, and a child who narrates day after day is learning to discern the main points of any given reading—another higher-level thinking skill. The mind must be active in order for a child to know:

> Most teachers know the dreariness of piles of exercises into which no stray note of personality has escaped. Now there is a natural provision against this mere skimming of the ground by the educational plough. Give children the sort of knowledge that they are fitted to assimilate, served in a literary medium, and they will pay great attention.... here we have a word of ancient wisdom for our guidance; "The mind can know nothing except what it can express in the form of an answer to a question put by the mind to itself." (*Philosophy of Education*, pp. 257–58)

The mental processes required by narration lay the foundation for scholarly habits of thinking. Narration is a sure path to real knowledge because it requires this process of self-questioning, and the daily practice of narration ensures that children grow and learn and think as they read their books.

Narration Develops Relationships

Beyond all this, narration is also a relationship-building activity. The act of narrating creates an environment in which a child is allowed to interact on a very personal level with what he has read, seen, or experienced. His narration allows him to focus on the parts that interested him—to relate what he has learned to other things that he knows—and at the very least to have the satisfaction of having made the acquaintance of some bit of knowledge.

Narration—telling about things—in everyday life is a kind of conversation that builds rapport and relationships with family, friends, and neighbors. Used consistently in education, narration builds the familiarity that encourages a child to care about what he is learning, and that caring is the basis of relationship, of ordering the affections. The beauty of this method is that it does its work even if the child does not enjoy the process of narrating, which is, after all, quite a mental effort. The relationships form in spite of his antipathy, and you will see evidence of this over time as a child will narrate spontaneously when his interest is sparked or connections are made.

Those of us who have been educating in this way for decades can only say "trust the process," which sounds arbitrary and uncertain, but which has proven itself true year after year. Like Miss Mason and Naaman's servant, we can only say: Please be willing to try this simple method. To the parent struggling with a first-time narrator, I can only say the same: Be consistent, and trust the process. I often add this: If you will not abandon narration, within three years, you will be giving this same advice to upcoming first-time narrators. It sounds like a long time, but with narration, we take the long view. Within three years, you will see some evidence of the power of narration in your own child, and when you do, I encourage you to share it with others so that the relationship-building method of narration will be established as an effective method, as widely practiced and respected as it deserves to be.

Fluent oral narrators learn to write their narrations and become fluent writers if the process is allowed to follow its full trajectory. Narration is a powerful educational method because it makes full use of an activity—telling about things—that is natural to us all. Miss Mason added narration to her principles of education because she came to see that this practice was indispensable to the working out of her principle that education is the science of relations. She fully appreciated the way in which narration fostered caring and relationships:

> The citizen in whose bringing-up P.N.E.U. has had a part has had
> many of his innumerable emotions stirred by his "lovely books,"
> "glorious books," and the emotion of the moment has translated
> the facts of history, travel, science, the themes of poetry or

tragedy, into vital knowledge. That is the *raison d'etre* of narrating; the reader recovers as it were what he has read and looks at it, and in this looking his emotion becomes fired. (Parents' National Educational Union, *In Memoriam*, pp. 11–12)

This is the experience of a young adult who narrated through his school years and then returned to the practice of narration for personal study. He recognized that narrating a book created a different, more relational experience:

> I started reading a dense and scholarly book—Eco's *Art and Beauty in the Middle Ages*—and I realized that I needed to narrate if I really wanted to understand and remember it. So I started narrating each chapter, and I found that this did two things. First, it forced me to think through what I had just read and make the ideas my own. No surprise there! Second—and this I wasn't expecting—it changed my mental attitude when I was reading, putting me into a more focused and receptive frame of mind.... It didn't just help my mind process and absorb what I had read after the fact. It reframed my relationship with the book from the outset, working like a plough, preparing my mental earth to receive the book even before I read it. (Testimony from *Know and Tell* by Karen Glass, p. 187)

Narration Produces Capable Learners

The last of these newly added practical principles underscores the need for a single reading and warns against practices that will hinder the primary objectives of education. Miss Mason insisted on a single reading for school books during school time because only under those conditions could the full attention of her pupils be secured. This is not a prohibition on rereading books another time or enjoying the same book over and over—she speaks elsewhere on the value of multiple readings of worthy books—but as an educational practice during lesson time, a single reading is important.

This practice is based upon the principle that children are born persons with capable minds, as we discussed earlier. If we believe in their ability to focus attention and recall the material in narration, then we have to make our practices match that belief, and we cannot undermine it by reading the material over again simply because a child did not pay attention. It's a hard thing to do, but the best practice is simply to express regret that the child missed something—let him feel that he missed it—and not to reread. The next time, he will have an incentive to pay attention, stimulated by the need to narrate. This is of greater value than the information missed in the lesson, which can be supplied later if it is needed. A child cannot narrate what he does not know, and he will not know unless he brings attention to bear. Narrating every day builds the power that is in him until attention becomes the intellectual habit we want it to be—the habit that will allow a more mature scholar to focus and grasp fully what he reads and hears. These practices that Miss Mason considered vital were included in the principles because they support the rest of those principles, and those who have used them have found her claims to be accurate.

This is the experience of a college graduate who was educated with these methods:

> In college, it shocked me to discover how poorly my classmates took notes, absorbed lectures, and studied for tests and papers. The ability to sit in a lecture, listen to the teacher, and emerge with new and useful information that fit neatly into what they already learned seemed to elude them. Eventually it dawned on me that the skill they were missing was the ability to read and listen with the intent to understand. To my surprise, I realized that the reason why I did have that skill was due to the countless narrations I had written. Every time I was presented with new information, I had trained myself to pay attention so that later on I could formulate an explanation of what I had learned. (Testimony from *Know and Tell*, p. 191)

Relationships Must Not Be Hindered

The fifteenth principle goes on to say that as well as rereading school lessons, there are a few other things to avoid—"questioning, summarising, and the like" (*Philosophy of Education*, p. xxx). It is important to understand the relationship of these practical principles to the dominant philosophical ones. If you don't grasp how all of this works together, you will lack the confidence to adhere to the methods that are best practices and give the most certain results.

For example, when you feel a child's narration is incomplete or too vague, there is a great temptation to begin asking questions. What was his name? Where did he live? Miss Mason knew how tempting it would be, so she included this warning in the very principles—don't do it. It is not an arbitrary prohibition. It undermines the process of narration in which a child's mind is required to deal with the material in its entirety and sift it for the order and details to narrate, finally shaping that into coherent sentences. There are natural narrators who narrate flawlessly from the very start, but most children need time to build their power and fluency. Questions like these interfere with the process, although it is always appropriate to ask for more and include a hint of what you'd like to hear in the question. For example, you might ask, "Can you tell me more about Benjamin's job with his brother?" or "Can you remember what happened during the first night?" Notice that these questions are not asking for specific details, and if the child cannot tell more, the narration is simply finished.

I have conducted a large-scale illustration of what intrusive questions that probe for specific information do to our thinking, and while it works best to experience it firsthand, I will try to describe it here. Miss Mason used narration in what she called "picture study," allowing a student to examine a picture—a work of fine art—and then narrate, giving as much detail about the picture as possible.

I began my illustration by showing a painting. I've used a few well-known works of art at different times, but which one does not matter. I let my audience look at the painting for a minute or so, removed it, and divided the group into two. I asked one half of the room to partner with someone next to them and narrate the painting. The room usually buzzed for half a minute or so, and then I stopped them and invited their listening partners to narrate any additional details they had noticed. Finally, I asked the group some kind of open-ended question. For example, I might ask, "If you were standing next to the artist while he painted this scene, what sounds might you have heard?" My question invited them to think "outside the frame."

Then, I turned my attention to the second group, who had been waiting patiently for the narrators to finish, and I told them they were going to have a different kind of activity based on the painting—I would ask them questions. I nearly always began by asking for some ridiculous detail that involved a number: "How many candles were in the boat? How many of them were lit?" Occasionally, someone knew the answer, but most of them didn't, and my questions made them feel foolish. I asked several more relatively inane questions, and then I asked them this: "Have I destroyed your interest in this picture?" The answer was usually yes. Questions about details and information are the opposite of relationship-building! Many children have been made to feel stupid because they cannot produce the answers to questions like these, and it destroys their love of learning.

I then invited both groups to imagine what would be going on in their minds the next time I set up a picture for picture study. The group that expected to narrate would be forming sentences in their minds as they looked at the picture. They would be searching for words to describe what they were seeing. The other group usually admitted they would be counting things because that is what I would be asking them about. Which of the two groups is more likely to develop a relationship with and find joy in pictures and art? Yet most traditional school exercises resemble those questions! Miss Mason lamented such practices "in which the mind may be bored and the affections deadened" (*Philosophy of Education*, p. 65).

Good Educational Practices Nurture the Growth of Relations

That is why we need to understand how the practices are related to the principles. We aren't merely concerned that the children remember some particular detail. That is not the object of education. We are shaping their mental processes—teaching them to observe and think and communicate—by the kinds of methods we use. Either we are helping them build relationships with knowledge, or we are hindering the formation of those relationships. That's why keeping the principle that *education is the science of relations* at the forefront of our thinking will safeguard us against these detrimental practices. Miss Mason wrote:

> The art of standing aside to let a child develop the relations proper to him is the fine art of education. (*School Education*, p. 67)

We must remember that what the teacher does for the child, the child will not do for himself. *Children are born persons* with capable minds, and these few practical principles include the reminder that they are based on the "behavior of mind" (*Philosophy of Education*, p. xxx)—the laws that govern how we think and learn. Our practices should be rooted firmly in our certainty that children are born persons who need to form their own relationships with knowledge. Supplying them with an abundance of excellent books and requiring them to narrate is a sure path to those relations. In the next three chapters, we will take a broad look at the way these principles work in each area of the curriculum.

11

Daily Bread: Knowledge of God

> We forget that it is written, Man shall not live by bread alone, but
> by every word that proceedeth out of the mouth of God shall man
> live,—whether it be spoken in the way of some truth of religion,
> poem, picture, scientific discovery, or literary expression; by
> these things men live and in all such is the life of the spirit. The
> spiritual life requires the food of ideas for its daily bread.
> —Charlotte Mason, *A Philosophy of Education*

Education Is the Pursuit of Wisdom and Virtue

When Charlotte Mason wrote about these practical principles in
Philosophy of Education, she offered by way of example the curriculum that the PNEU was using. However, she did not lose sight of the
larger picture while working out practical details, and neither should
we. Every practice is grounded in the context of the principles that
children are born persons and *education is the science of relations*, along
with all their corollary principles. It is more important to understand
the connection of each area of study to the principles than to focus
on specific books or curriculum, although that will be necessary as
well. Remember that when we understand principles, they govern our
actions. Miss Mason explained:

> I venture to propose one or two principles in the matter of school-
> books, and shall leave the far more difficult part, the application
> of those principles, to the reader. (*School Education*, p. 177)

In the next few chapters, we will look at all the different areas of
study in order to understand the relationship between each subject

and the principles. This will lay the foundation for being able to make practical choices about books and curriculum. I have not included detailed "how to" descriptions for each subject because there is no space for this. Instead, I have tried to link each area of study to the ideas that govern it. Practical application may be found elsewhere,* but understanding the harmony of ideas with the school subjects may be more fruitful than practical suggestions. Miss Mason celebrated the practical nature of ideas:

> Nothing is so practical as a great idea, because nothing produces such an abundant outcome of practical effort. We must not turn the cold shoulder to philosophy. Education is no more than applied philosophy—our effort to train children according to the wisdom that is in us; and not according to the last novelty in educational ideas. (*School Education*, p. 118)

We must remember that *education is the science of relations* is a many-layered way of describing what Miss Mason called *wisdom*. As we saw in chapter 3, she linked wisdom to natural philosophy, moral philosophy, and religion and asserted, "In this science of the relations of things consists what we call wisdom" (*Parents and Children*, pp. 258–59).

All these areas of wisdom or philosophy begin in wonder—in a natural appreciation, awe, and curiosity about everything there is to know. Children come into the world with this wonder, but it is easily lost when they are subjected to deadly educational practices like the inane questions I described earlier—and to a child full of awe and wonder, most questions are inane. Our educational practices should be shaped to preserve and encourage their healthy appetite for knowledge. The world is teeming with interesting things to learn about, and it is the occupation of a person to form as many relationships as possible. Our teaching methods should be rooted in our firm belief that children are born persons and that our task as teachers is to introduce them to many vital relationships.

---

* Two useful books that teach practical application of these methods in various subjects are *A Charlotte Mason Education* by Catherine Levison and *A Charlotte Mason Companion* by Karen Andreola. In addition, many practical applications are explained at *www.amblesideonline.org*.

In this discussion, Miss Mason used terms that were familiar in the history of thought about education. She equated wisdom with philosophy, and this recalls a tradition that goes back to ancient Greece, where philosophy was the object of learning:

> By joining *philia* (love) with *sophia* (wisdom) the ancients held together what we moderns often separate, namely, the seemingly subjective quality of love with the often objectified idea of truth. However, the ancients understood that it is not enough merely to possess wisdom—as if one could in fact possess knowledge purely objectively or dispassionately—one must actually love it and pursue it from the soul. (Clark and Jain, *The Liberal Arts Tradition*, p. 83)

This is essentially what we understand by the principle that *education is the science of relations*—we must learn to care about many things. Tradition divides philosophy into several branches, some of which Miss Mason mentioned in her discussion: natural philosophy, moral philosophy, and divine philosophy. Each represents a relationship with a different aspect of reality, and the methods we employ will either help or hinder the formation of those relationships.

Natural philosophy is concerned with the physical world. Moral philosophy is concerned with the nature and purpose of man and how that reality should govern our behavior. Divine philosophy might be equated with religion, but its sphere of understanding concerns transcendent truth and reality that is beyond the physical world—metaphysics. Truth, goodness, and beauty belong to this realm. These are heady topics—the subjects of centuries of philosophical pursuit—and they might seem beyond the reach of ordinary teachers or the children they are teaching. But that is not at all the case.

Miss Mason was convinced that a liberal education was for everyone, and she believed it possible that "the souls of all children are waiting for the call of knowledge to awaken them to delightful living" (*Philosophy of Education*, p. xxv). She had seen children from severely underprivileged backgrounds thrive on this rich exposure to knowledge, and it gave her confidence to declare that "these principles and methods make education entirely effectual" (*Philosophy of Education*, p. xxvii).

Key Ideas Initiate Each Area of Study

In chapter 3, we saw that Miss Mason considered the principle that *education is the science of relations* to be the "captain idea" that should guide educational thinking. In a similar vein, she believed that a captain idea should govern our approach to each area of the curriculum:

> Every subject has its living way, with what Coleridge calls "its guiding idea" at the head, and it is only as we discover this living way in each case that a subject of instruction makes for the education of a child. (*Parents and Children*, p. 279)

> Every relation must be *initiated* by its own "captain" idea, sustained upon fitting ideas; and wrought into the material substance of the *person* by its proper habits. (*School Education*, p. 71, emphasis added)

The captain idea in each subject should quicken imagination because it is a living thought—an idea-seed that may sprout and bear fruit if it is planted and tended well. At the head of each area of study discussed in these "Daily Bread" chapters, I have included a captain idea from the chapter titled "The Curriculum" in *A Philosophy of Education*—an idea that draws from each subject one of its living seeds, the life-giving ideas that it brings to a child's education. This is where each subject begins, and then within each topic, there is work to be done on two fronts: ideas and habits.

> Two main principles are—the recognition of the physical basis of habit, *i.e.*, of the material side of education; and of the inspiring and formative power of ideas, *i.e.*, of the immaterial, or spiritual, side of education. These two guiding principles, covering as they do the whole field of human nature, should enable us to deal rationally with all the complex problems of education. (*Parents and Children*, preface)

Each area of the curriculum has ideas to offer a child that will enlarge his soul and invite him to care about some particular things. Upon the ideas, habits of thinking and acting can be formed that lay the foundation of a virtuous life. For example, a child who learns to appreciate the life cycle of honeybees or butterflies has the seed of an idea that will perhaps prevent him from treating any animal cruelly. A child who watches Benjamin Franklin grow up in a biography may be inspired to take initiative and work hard in his own endeavors. As educators, we cannot know exactly which ideas will catch hold of the mind of each child, and that is why our task is simply to spread a generous feast that will include something for everyone.

With the fullest appreciation for the scope of what education is meant to be and what it is meant to accomplish in the life of a person, Miss Mason listed all the different parts of curriculum under the three great areas of relationship—Knowledge of God (divine philosophy), Knowledge of Man (moral philosophy), and Knowledge of the Universe (natural philosophy). This chapter and the two following chapters discuss the various areas of the curriculum that fall under these headings. Because we are persons, wisdom and the virtue it inspires are exactly the things we should pursue in every area of study. We begin with the knowledge of God, which is governed by the captain idea:

> The expressed knowledge attainable by us has its source in the Bible, and perhaps we cannot do a greater indignity to children than to substitute our own or some other benevolent person's rendering for the fine English, poetic diction and lucid statement of the Bible. (*Philosophy of Education*, p. 160)

School Lessons Supplement Home Teaching of the Bible

Miss Mason considered the knowledge of God of primary importance. This relationship is, of course, the profound relationship of life. She was rather blunt when she said that if this is denied, she wasn't even sure how the proper conditions of teaching and learning could operate:

> I am assuming that everyone entrusted with the bringing up of children recognises the supreme Authority to Whom we are subject; without this recognition I do not see how it is possible to establish the nice relation which should exist between teacher and taught. (*Philosophy of Education*, p. 73)

A relationship with God as a loving Father is beyond the scope of a school classroom, where a teacher can only hope to supplement the teaching of home and church. Miss Mason was quite definite that "mothers are on the whole more successful in communicating this knowledge than are teachers" (*Philosophy of Education*, p. 158). The knowledge of higher things unfolds gradually to a child who lives in the atmosphere of a home where God is loved, honored, and served.

However, within the scope of school lessons, Miss Mason wanted her pupils to read both the Old Testament and the New Testament. The Old Testament provides us with a picture of the relationship between God and man, and the New Testament is based upon that picture.

> Let us have faith and courage to give children such a full and gradual picture of Old Testament history that they unconsciously perceive for themselves a panoramic view of the history of mankind typified by that of the Jewish nation as it is unfolded in the Bible. (*Philosophy of Education*, p. 162)

The Bible Is the Primary Text

Because the object of this study is a broad knowledge of the way that God deals with men, the primary method of lessons is simply reading and narrating through the Bible (with necessary omissions according to a child's age and maturity). Miss Mason included reading from commentaries as "background for their thoughts" (*Philosophy of Education*, p. 163), but the focus of the lesson was Scripture itself, preferably the Authorized [King James] Version for its "fine English and poetic diction" (*Philosophy of Education*, p. 160).

She hoped that a child would read through the Old Testament two or three times during his school career. The first time, when he was young, it would be read to him over the course of several years, and the second time (beginning around age twelve), he would read it through for himself. This might be followed by a third time if his formal schooling continued until age seventeen or eighteen. The focus of this school reading is the knowledge of God that is found in the Bible.

Miss Mason suggested age-appropriate commentaries for each level of reading that focused on the geographical and historical background that would illuminate the reading without superseding it. She was well aware of the criticism of biblical texts that led to dismissing Old Testament stories as false. Her desire was to preserve reverence for God's Word without shrinking from modern criticism:

They leave school with a fairly enlightened knowledge of the books of the Old Testament and of the aids modern scholarship has brought towards their interpretation; we hope also with increased reverence for and delight in the ways of God with men. (*Philosophy of Education*, p. 165)

While the reading of the Old Testament focuses on God's dealings with men, the New Testament reading should focus on the life and teaching of Jesus Christ found in the first three Gospels. Miss Mason reserved the reading of the Gospel of John and Acts for high school and the epistles and Revelation for the final year or two of school. This allows many years for observing and learning about God through the person of Jesus Christ alone.

The Focus Is on Relationships

The method of lessons is simple and consistent—Bible passages are read and narrated. Miss Mason was aware of the temptation to draw out a moral lesson or make a personal application. She was quite definite that "very little hortatory teaching is desirable" and "the danger of boring young listeners by such teaching is great" (*Philosophy of Education*, p. 166). In order to forestall this practice, she tried to give teachers a vision of the kind of knowledge she hoped students would gain by simply reading and narrating.

By degrees the Person of Our Lord as revealed in His words and His works becomes real and dear to them, not through emotional appeals but through the impression left by accurate and detailed knowledge concerning the Saviour of the World, Who went about doing good. Dogmatic teaching finds its way to them by inference through a quiet realisation of the Bible records; and loyalty to a Divine Master is likely to become the guiding principle of their lives. (*Philosophy of Education*, p. 165)

If you remember that narration is a relationship-building practice, it will be easier to allow the child to have this direct access to the Bible narrative without additions from outside. Miss Mason urged what she called a "poetic presentation" of the life of Christ. She did not mean children should read poetry instead of the Bible narrative (although she did have her older pupils read her own poetic rendering, *The Saviour of the World*, along with the biblical text). Rather, a poetic, relational understanding of the material should encourage "a delightful sense of harmonious development, of the rounding out of each incident, of the progressive unfolding which characterises our Lord's teaching" (*Philosophy of Education*, pp. 165–66). She affirmed the importance of narration because "the custom of narration lends itself surprisingly to this sort of poetic insight" (*Philosophy of Education*, p. 166).

If we spend some time pondering Miss Mason's ideas about the way Bible lessons should be conducted and why she used this method, it will provide a window of insight into all the other areas of the curriculum. It is grounded in her principles of education. Because *children are born persons*, they are spiritual beings with capable minds. Because *education is the science of relations*, only those relationships that they develop or perceive for themselves are of use to them as persons.

With Bible teaching, Miss Mason selected two guiding ideas to shape her approach to Scripture. She wanted her students to perceive the way that God works in men's lives in the Old Testament, and she wanted them to develop a personal appreciation and love for Christ by reading the New Testament. These are relational objectives, and she was willing to allow the relationship-building activity of narration to be the foundation on which the relationships grow.

Keeping these simple ideas in mind, we can look at all the areas of the curriculum and perceive the way in which Miss Mason was absolutely consistent in her belief that children were able to form relationships for their own sakes and learn to find delight in all areas of knowledge.

Things to Remember about Teaching Bible

1. Read through the whole of the Bible and supplement with background material that illuminates the Bible passage.
2. Use narration because it encourages a poetic appreciation of the readings.
3. Allow the text to do its own teaching without insisting upon personal application.

12

Daily Bread: Knowledge of Man

And there are some few ideas which are as the daily bread of the
soul, without which life and growth are impossible.
—Charlotte Mason, *Home Education*

As I shared earlier, "knowledge of man" includes all the things that
fall under the heading of moral philosophy. While we are still dealing
with young children, we are not concerned with the highest levels
of philosophical understanding, but we are, nevertheless, laying the
foundation for that understanding. Within this category, in various
areas of the curriculum, children will encounter the ideas that will
shape their understanding of who man is and what his duties are,
and they will also find inspiration that we hope will shape their own
choices and actions.

As persons, we are born with consciences that want to do right, but
we are essentially ignorant of what is right and what is wrong. The
studies in this category educate our consciences and teach us how to
make right choices. These studies will not make children virtuous,
but if we teach them well, they will have a good idea of what virtue
looks like and how it behaves.

History

*It is necessary to know something of what has gone before in order to
think justly of what is occurring today.*

Children Begin a Relationship with Time and Long Ago

The two principles that govern the study of history are the same
two that guide everything else—*children are born persons* and *education is the science of relations.* Through the study of history, persons can
develop a relationship with the persons who have lived before.

My generation grew up with a scrappy knowledge of history. It
was not a designated subject in schools (we had social studies), and
history seemed to be random stories—the *Mayflower*, Christopher
Columbus, George Washington—that were completely unconnected.
The idea of history generally represented a sort of soup called "a long
time ago," and the ingredients just swirled together unless we pulled
one out on a spoon for a moment. But in a pot of soup, the carrots,
the potatoes, the peas, and the onions all taste pretty much the same,
and no strong sense of history was ever my possession until I started
homeschooling my children, and we learned it together.

Many home teachers share my story—we didn't learn history as
children, and when we did learn it as adults, we were extremely
excited about all the connections we had missed as children. It is very
easy to fall into the mistake of assuming that our children, getting
something we did not, will apprehend history in the same way we
do. We must curb our enthusiasm and allow them to build their own
relationships.

Children—especially children under the age of ten—do not have a
strong sense of time. Many six-year-olds are still learning the days of
the week and the months of the year. They do not have a firm grasp
of living from January to December again and again and again, and
therefore, they have no clear sense of what a year means. A year is a
vast expanse of time in which there will be a birthday, a Christmas, a
vacation, a summer, a winter, and a Fourth of July fireworks display,
and all of these things will occur at great intervals, between which
there will be long successions of ordinary days. Children live in the

present, and last Christmas and next birthday are not a matter of a few short months as they are to us adults.

We need to understand this as we teach them history. When you go to your doctor and have blood work done, you might receive the results on a piece of paper littered with what appear to be random, meaningless numbers. You will probably hand it back to your doctor and ask, "What does this mean?"

A timeline presents a similar puzzle to a young child. They need to experience a little more time for themselves before they can begin to distinguish centuries and decades and realize that no, Grandpa wasn't alive at the same time as Moses. This doesn't mean we won't use the timelines, because they are an important tool in the process of learning, but we need to remember that our children will not immediately understand them as we do. Miss Mason encouraged the use of different kinds of history timelines and notebooks to build their understanding gradually. Their personal notebooks "nurture the science of relations" (Laurie Bestvater, *The Living Page*, p. xv).

We Should Learn History Chronologically

So what do we want our history studies to accomplish? Remember that *education is the science of relations*. We want our children to get to know a person—a historical person—or get a sense of what life was like for a certain group of people in a particular place a long time ago. Because "a long time ago" is so abstract, children will begin to understand it better if they start in one definite place and move forward in their studies as time moves forward. Therefore, Charlotte Mason had her students study history chronologically rather than in the random bits of my childhood.

The chronological study of history has become a popular way of organizing school studies in the homeschooling community, as well as in many schools. However, history is not the only way to organize studies, and we make a mistake if we make a shibboleth of teaching history "from beginning to end." Every child need not begin at the beginning. Chronology can begin wherever it is convenient to start. The point is to study history wisely and in order, but Miss Mason wanted children to "grip where they alight." That firm grasp on a beginning point, followed by steady progress forward, is more important than the precise bit of history in which he begins.

> Historical and scientific subjects have only a nominal beginning, the important thing is that children should grip where they alight, should take hold of the subject with keen interest, and then in time they will feel their own way backwards and forwards. ("Parents' Review School" in *The Parents' Review*, volume 12)

We Should Learn History for Character

Rather than focusing on the nonessential question of when history should begin, or even whether or not American children should begin only with the history of America, let us consider the real purpose of our history studies, which is not merely the acquisition of specific knowledge.

> Here, too, is a subject which should be to the child an inexhaustible storehouse of ideas, should enrich the chambers of his [mind] with a thousand tableaux, pathetic and heroic, and should form in him, insensibly, principles whereby he will hereafter judge of the behaviour of nations, and will rule his own conduct as one of a nation. This is what the study of history should do for the child. (*Home Education*, p. 279)

With that picture before us of what history should offer a child, all the other questions become quite secondary. It will make no difference to the child at all where he begins with his history studies. The approach we take, however, makes all the difference in the world, and the wrong way of studying history can be detrimental. Miss Mason deplored the reading of a "miserable little chronicle" (*Home Education*, p. 279) of history that is focused on the succession of one person after another and governed by dates that mean little to a child yet.

> No way of warping the judgment of the child, of filling him with crude notions, narrow prejudices, is more successful than that of carrying him through some such course of English history; and all the more so if his little text-book be moral or religious in tone, and undertake to point the moral as well as to record the fact. Moral teaching falls, no doubt, within the province of history; but the one small volume which the child uses affords no scope for

the fair and reasonable discussion upon which moral decisions should be based, nor is the child old enough to be put into the judicial attitude which such a decision supposes. (*Home Education*, p. 280)

Because so much of history is political—something well beyond the grasp of small children—Miss Mason felt that it was more appropriate to begin with the history and tales of the heroic age. Kings and enemies, tales of bravery and heroism, or tales of honor and sacrifice have an appeal that political agendas and strategic alliances simply never will.

This makes a book about golden deeds of history an excellent early history book. As you read each story, you can add them to a timeline— it does help to build a sense of time—but the exposure to heroic acts is the more vital part of the history reading. Another good beginning point is a biography, especially if it is well written, about a memorable person such as Benjamin Franklin or George Washington. As children get to know one person, they also get a sense of the historical era in which he lived, unfettered by dates or agendas.

We Must Learn from History before We Judge

We have a tendency to vilify historical figures by pronouncing judgment on them according to our own cultural values. We should take note of Miss Mason's warning that the child is "not old enough to be put into the judicial attitude" (*Home Education*, p. 280). Children need to believe in heroes—to believe that a person can perform a great task, take a great risk, overcome a fearsome foe or a great hardship, and emerge victorious.

Just as we may mistakenly expect our children to understand the relationships of time before they are ready, we may also expect a balanced understanding that they are too immature to possess. As adults we know heroes are flawed—sometimes badly. But with our adult perspective—knowing that we, too, are flawed in some ways—we can still appreciate a person's accomplishments.

Children will figure out that heroes are flawed when they grow up—probably long before they are fully grown. They won't be able to help it. But if they have first learned that a person can be heroic, the logical conclusion is that flawed people can do great things. If imperfect people cannot be heroes, then there are no heroes at all—and the world always needs heroes. If our criterion is that heroes must be unflawed, then there are no heroes. There never have been. And more importantly, there never will be any more.

The child who becomes a cynical judge of human nature in first grade—who learns only that men are flawed, but not that they can be heroes—will never aspire to be one. He will not dream of sacrificing his own safety and well-being for the sake of others. He will not risk ridicule by taking a stand in a worthy cause. He will not set out on a quest to achieve a great task.

It is only when children are young that untarnished heroism is possible for them. Of course, they will learn later that their heroes were not always perfect, but when they do, they will have a better understanding of human nature, and their knowledge will be tempered with mercy. Just as they will grow into a better understanding about ages of time, they will grow into a fuller appreciation of human nature.

Miss Mason referenced a quote from John Stuart Mill that underscores this point:

> "But before we teach children to criticise the institutions of their country, before we teach them to be critical of what is bad, let us teach them to recognize and admire what is good. After all life is very short; we all of us have only one life to live, and during that life let us get into ourselves as much love, as much admiration, as much elevating pleasure as we can, and if we view education merely as discipline in critical bitterness, then we shall lose all the sweets of life and we shall make ourselves unnecessarily miserable. There is quite enough sorrow and hardship in this world as it is without introducing it prematurely to young people." (quoted in *Philosophy of Education*, p. 126)

This is a reminder to us that *education is the science of relations*. Learn to love and care first, and criticism and judgment can come later. Miss Mason had a vision for what history should provide students:

> It is a great thing to possess a pageant of history in the background of one's thoughts. We may not be able to recall this or that circumstance, but, "the imagination is warmed"; we know that

there is a great deal to be said on both sides of every question and are saved from crudities in opinion and rashness in action. The present becomes enriched for us with the wealth of all that has gone before. (*Philosophy of Education*, p. 178)

Our Approach to History Is Governed by Relationships

When we understand exactly what the study of history should provide for persons of mind and conscience, we will not mistake what is essential and what is not. As I mentioned earlier, the exact starting place for history is largely irrelevant, except as we choose history that will appeal to the heroic impulse of our children. The attitude we take toward what we study and the chronological reading that will allow the "pageant" to develop and progress are more important. It is not an easy thing to give up our desire that the children will "recall this or that circumstance," but narration and the use of a timeline or book of centuries* (a special kind of timeline used in the PNEU) will provide the framework that keeps the vital aspects of history accessible to our students.

Because children are persons, our object with history studies is to help them form a relationship with other times and the people who lived in those times, and our purpose is not merely for the sake of knowing important historical dates or people that it would be a shame not to know. That knowledge will take care of itself by the way if we keep the primary purpose of educating the conscience of a child in mind. As a person, he must make choices about right and wrong, and history will provide him with a wealth of examples of similar choices from which to learn. Once the foundation is laid in the early years, Miss Mason recommended consecutive reading through an excellent volume of the history of one's own country, accompanied by the contemporary history of other countries for the broadest possible perspective.

> Perhaps the gravest defect in school curricula is that they fail to give a comprehensive, intelligent and interesting introduction to history. To leave off or even to begin with the history of our own country is fatal. We can not live sanely unless we know that other

---

* For thorough discussion about the way these books were used in PNEU schools, I recommend reading *The Living Page* by Laurie Bestvater.

peoples are as we are with a difference, that their history is as ours, with a difference, that they too have been represented by their poets and their artists, that they too have their literature and their national life. (*Philosophy of Education*, p. 178)

This background of history offers children material that will help them in their work as persons when they must make choices, giving them "those two ratifiers and props of every present word and action, Antiquity and Custom" that will inform their decisions. The knowledge of history is important to a person because it will "give weight to his decisions, consideration to his actions and stability to his conduct" (*Philosophy of Education*, p. 179).

Miss Mason said, "Right thinking was the most important act in a man's life. If he thought right he would act right." (Cholmondeley, *The Story of Charlotte Mason*, p. 66). History offers a child some of that material of right thinking that will help to form his own character.

Things to Remember about Teaching History

1. Study history to learn about human character.
2. Study chronologically in order to see the consequences of ideas and actions.
3. Rather than passing judgment on history, let history studies inform our judgment about current decisions.

Literature

Literature "feeds a child's sense of wonder" and great tales "find their way to children's hearts."

Books Feed Our Hearts

We ask multiple things of literature in the curriculum. Stories reach a child's heart through his imagination. Because of this direct path to something so precious, we should take care that the stories we give children are grounded in truth, goodness, and beauty. This does not mean that their books should be overtly moralistic. In fact, the opposite is true. The truths of the world—both good and bad— should reach them cushioned by the beauty, grandeur, and pathos of a story well told.

The books children read are building their moral imagination so that they will be able to empathize with people in all kinds of circumstance. Their books should have the flavor of heroism, victory, sacrifice, and redemption. The books they read are giving them a picture of the way the world operates and what is possible for them in that world. The truth is that there is evil in the world, and the further truth is that evil has been overcome. That reality seeps into their consciousness little by little through the stories they read, and they will begin to comprehend that they too have a part to play in the great story that is life.

Miss Mason knew that literature develops children's imaginations in this way and that it can motivate them to generous action:

> Let them have tales of the imagination, scenes laid in other lands and other times, heroic adventures, hairbreadth escapes, delicious fairy tales in which they are never roughly pulled up by the impossible—even where all is impossible, and they know it, and yet believe.
>
> ...It is not impossible that posterity may write us down a generation blest with little imagination, and, by so far, the less capable of great conceptions and heroic efforts, for it is only as we have it in us to let a person or a cause fill the whole stage of the mind, to the exclusion of self occupation, that we are capable of large hearted action on behalf of that person or cause.
>
> ...The children should have the joy of living in far lands, in other persons, in other times—a delightful double existence; and this joy they will find, for the most part, in their story books. (*Home Education*, pp. 152–53)

Reading imaginative literature is formative for children. Because the teaching is not didactic but woven into stories that captivate them, lessons of goodness and love and heroism reach their hearts. It is through stories that children learn to love the virtues of truth, justice, perseverance, and service.

Books Are Our Teachers

The standards for literature in this educational paradigm are high. When we look at the books that Miss Mason mentions as examples, we may discover that she gave nine-year-olds a book to read that many people don't read until high school. There is also the possibility, since most of us grew up in fairly weak institutional schools, that she gave books to nine-year-olds that we have not read yet and are a little scared of as adults.

If you've been exploring this educational method for even a short time, you've probably already discovered that no one needs this kind of education more than you do, yourself. And that's okay. Many educators have walked that path before you, and the collective advice is generally to jump right in—the water's fine. You will find that a difficult book grows easier as you go through it because the book is the teacher that will teach you how to read it. If you will submit yourself to the discipline of reading short portions and narrating them with your child (who may find the book far less daunting than you do), you will be stretched, and you will grow—as will your child.

This is an area where the principle that *children are born persons* with capable minds that can digest literary language must be grasped with both hands. Hold on tightly to that principle and jump into the book, trusting the law to work as you trust gravity to hold you to the ground. "Believe in mind" urged Miss Mason, and I can only echo her words. *Believe* in it. Believe that you can begin reading a difficult book that you scarcely understand and that your child apparently hates, and believe that when you are finished, the final chapter will be perfectly understandable. It is even conceivable that your child will name the book as one of his favorites. I'm not promising it will happen exactly like that. I'm simply saying believe that it's possible because it is, and hundreds of parents and teachers who made that leap of faith can testify that it is so.

Can six- and seven-year-olds enjoy a seventeenth-century classic like *Pilgrim's Progress?* Yes, they can. Can nine-year-olds follow *Robinson Crusoe?* I know they are doing it every year. Can twelve-year-olds read *Ivanhoe?* Most certainly. This is all possible. Just as Miss Mason didn't hesitate to offer her experience with PNEU students to illustrate her methods, I can also share from experience. As one of the designers of AmblesideOnline curriculum, which is based on Miss Mason's principles and modeled after PNEU programs, for nearly twenty years I have seen students and their parents respond to literature exactly as she told us they would.

All children show the same surprising power of knowing, evinced by the one sure test,—they are able to "tell" each work they have read not only with accuracy but with spirit and originality.... They see it all so vividly that when you read or hear their versions the theme is illuminated for you too. (*Philosophy of Education*, p. 182)

Literature Corresponds to History and Informs Conduct

When possible, assign literature that was written in the time period being studied in history. Students learning the history of the Middle Ages will read *Beowulf* and *The Canterbury Tales*. Students studying the Civil War era will read *Uncle Tom's Cabin* and *Adventures of Huckleberry Finn*. Those studying twentieth-century history will read *Animal Farm* and *Fahrenheit 451*. The purpose of this correlation, which should not be carried to excess or followed slavishly, is to illustrate the nature of the ideas prevalent in the time period being studied. The literature of an age mirrors the thoughts of that age.

It is tempting to offer easier, modern literature to students, but it is a temptation we should resist in school lessons, although they can enjoy newer books during their free time. The literature our students read because it is assigned is shaping their taste and giving them a larger capacity for thinking and future learning. To this end, a challenging book that must be read in small portions and narrated over many weeks can be formative. If the work is chosen well, it will contain examples of life and living that inform those "principles of conduct," called for in the nineteenth principle, that we want to give our students. It doesn't mean every character will be a good example, but the right kind of book will illustrate life and character in some way.

A fluent nine-year-old reader could read through every book in the latest popular series and be not one bit the better person. If the same nine-year-old read through just one excellent book—perhaps *Little Women* or *Robinson Crusoe*—ideas about character and living and dying and personal sacrifice and service for others will at least have had a chance to be planted as seeds that might grow to shape his character.

Quality, not quantity, is the object with literature. Miss Mason did not hesitate to call what she was offering children a feast, but she was not in favor of extensive light reading:

> Novels are our lesson-books only so far as we give thoughtful, considerate reading to such novels as are also literature. The young person who reads three books a week...is not likely to find in any of them "example of life and instruction in manners." These things arrive to us after many readings of a book that is worth while. (*Formation of Character*, pp. 373–74)

For that reason, the literature that is included in school reading should be of the very highest quality, and lesser books should be reserved for free time. Miss Mason wanted us to spend time on the best literature because of its influence on our moral imagination:

> Whether it be for a year or a life, let us mark as we read, let us learn and inwardly digest. Note how good this last word is. What we digest we assimilate, take into ourselves, so that it is part and parcel of us, and no longer separable.
>
> We probably read Shakespeare in the first place for his stories, afterwards for his characters, the multitude of delightful persons with whom he makes us so intimate that afterwards, in fiction or in fact, we say, "She is another Jessica," and "That dear girl is a Miranda"; "She is a Cordelia to her father," and, such a figure in history, "a base Iago." To become intimate with Shakespeare in this way is a great enrichment of mind and *instruction of conscience*. Then, by degrees, as we go on reading this world-teacher, lines of insight and beauty take possession of us, and unconsciously mould our judgments of men and things and of the great issues of life. (*Ourselves*, Book II, p. 72, emphasis added)

Our approach to literature in education should be governed by the principle that children are persons who will be responsible for choosing to act for good or evil, and the better they understand human nature, the stronger will be their foundation for making right choices. Being careful to choose excellent literature is a part of educating a child's conscience. The literature that he reads will expand his horizons to include a host of affairs and characters. That broad exposure will help him understand other people, and his own character and conduct will be fortified by their experiences.

Things to Remember about Teaching Literature

1. Choose excellent literature and trust children to grow into it.
2. Take your time with a few excellent books rather than trying to read too many things.
3. Allow children to digest and narrate and form their own relationships with the literature that they read.

Citizenship (Morals and Economics)

Children begin to gather conclusions as to the general life of the community.

Children Need to Understand Their Place in Community

Miss Mason used the broad heading of "citizenship" to cover a number of the relations that fall under the heading "knowledge of man." She mentions morals and economics, which seem like very different things, but perhaps they are not. Bearing in mind that we are all persons living in a world governed by the order of laws that operate in all our interactions with each other, we need to form an acquaintance with those laws. What are the duties incumbent upon us as members of a family, a community, a state? What are our responsibilities toward others both in our close relations and in our wider ones? How should we handle our civic duties, our finances, and our property? It should not surprise us that this area of study, like the rest, is primarily for the purpose of helping children to think rightly so that they might act rightly.

> In giving children the knowledge of men and affairs which we class under "Citizenship" we have to face the problem of good and evil. (*Philosophy of Education*, p. 186)

Miss Mason liked to use Plutarch's *Lives* to cover this subject. These lives are the biographies of one man at a time, so there is a personal element—the possibility of a relational interest in the subject. The lives that Plutarch shared with us are the lives of ancient Greeks or Romans who lived and acted in community. They employed their wills in the service of others, or else they were motivated by their personal desires. Plutarch told us what they did and the consequences that resulted from their actions. According to Miss Mason, this was a good way to give young people "principles of conduct." She wanted children to see what ambition could lead to or how much good could be done by a man who gave himself up to serve his country. Plutarch showed the strengths and weaknesses of his subjects, and all this was fodder for studies in the community relationships of life:

> The boy, or girl, aged from ten to twelve, who is intimate with a dozen or so of Plutarch's *Lives*, so intimate that *they influence his thought and conduct*, has learned to put his country first and to see individuals only as they serve or dis-serve the State. Thus he gets his first lesson in the science of proportion. Children familiar with the great idea of a State in the sense, not of a government but of the people, learn readily enough about the laws, customs and government of their country; learn, too, with great interest something about themselves, mind and body, heart and soul, because they feel it is well to know what they have it in them to give to their country. (*Philosophy of Education*, p. 187, emphasis added)

Children Can Make Application for Themselves

The manner of teaching citizenship was the same as it generally is in this educational paradigm—the children read (or are read to), and then they narrate what they have read. Miss Mason showed us that children draw their own conclusions and make their own applications from this reading:

> "Oh dear," said a little girl coming out of a swimming bath, "I'm just like Julius Caesar, I don't care to do a thing at all if I'm not best at it." So, in unlikely ways and from unlikely sources, do children gather that little code of principles which shall guide their lives. (*Philosophy of Education*, p. 189)

Miss Mason offered Plutarch as an example of someone who had himself learned insight into human character from his reading:

> The father of Plutarch had him learn his Homer that he might get heroic ideas of life. Had the boy been put through his Homer as a classical grind, as a machine for the development of faculty, a pedant would have come out, and not a man of the world in touch with life at many points, capable of bringing men and affairs to

the touchstone of a sane and generous mind. (*School Education*, pp. 151–52)

Plutarch read literature not as matter for critical study but to get ideas about life and character. Miss Mason believed that was the reason he was able to comprehend and portray the men he wrote about with so much sympathy and wisdom. It is a strong hint for us that it is not just what we read but also how we read it that makes an impact on us.

If we follow Miss Mason's lead, it matters most that we learn to read—Plutarch, literature, history, and everything else—in the right frame of mind. Our posture and attitude matter. We must read for relationships—to get ideas for life. This allows us to glean from our studies the things that are most worth learning—not the details of the time and the place but what motivated this person to act in this way and what the outcome was. A child's study of citizenship should have an effect on his character.

Things to Remember about Teaching Citizenship

1. Education should provide us with principles of conduct for virtuous actions.
2. Our reading should be focused on the ideas that are illustrated.
3. Both good and bad examples can be educational for us.

Composition

*Composition is something children
"are richly endowed to do for themselves."*

Composition Is Based on Narration

Our current crisis of education, in which far too few children learn to write well, is a cause for much concern. This was less true in Miss Mason's time, and as a consequence, her remarks on composition do not always feel adequate in the twenty-first century. For her oldest pupils, she said:

> Some definite teaching in the art of composition is advisable, but
> not too much, lest the young scholars be saddled with a stilted
> style which may encumber them for life. (*Philosophy of Education*,
> p. 193)

However, she did not give us many practical suggestions for this
definite teaching. That does not mean her methods or principles are
inadequate. If they are sound, we can still apply them to our own time
and needs. Composition is a natural extension of narration, which is
exercised in all areas of the curriculum. Every time children narrate,
they are practicing the art of composition, and this is the foundation
for excellent writing skills.

After using narration from start to finish with my own children
and observing hundreds of others doing the same, I have come to
see that narration has four stages which overlap and flow naturally
from one into the other. The first stage is oral fluency, in which
children learn to tell back very thoroughly what they have read or
heard. The second stage is written fluency, in which children begin
to write their narrations, although at this stage their writing resem-
bles their spoken narrations and has no prescribed form. The third
stage is composition, in which the written narrations are constructed
according to accepted standards in writing, and the fourth stage is
formal writing, in which the fluent narrator learns to produce papers
on demand in whatever form they are required, such as an objective
précis or a persuasive essay. I have written extensively on this topic
in another book, *Know and Tell: The Art of Narration*.

Composition Is Governed by the Principles of Persons and Relations

The methods used for teaching and growing the skill of composition
are based in the principles. We are relationship-forming persons, and
narration encourages those relationships. From the very beginning of
their school years, children practice oral composition as they narrate.
When they are ready, they begin writing narrations as well. Once they
can produce fluent written narrations, they begin composition with
the idea of communication already inherent in their minds. Because
they are used to narrating *to* someone, they understand that there is
an audience. This is an important relational aspect of composition.

Every piece of writing has an audience. Who is that audience? A writer bears his relationship to his audience in mind as he writes and chooses the best form of communication for the occasion. Does he want to inform his audience? To persuade them? To entertain them? This relational understanding of composition underlies the various types of writing we ask our students to do and gives them a solid foundation for writing effectively.

The common approach to composition can be sterile and artificial. Miss Mason deplored exercises that coached children through the process of writing a paper in tedious, detailed steps. She gave an example of an exercise meant to help children write a composition about umbrellas by answering mundane questions about what it was made of and how it was used. She would not have appreciated the modern trend of building a paragraph sentence by tortured sentence.

> A few years ago the appalling discovery was made that, both in secondary and elementary schools, "composition" was dreadfully defective, and, therefore, badly taught. Since then many volumes have been produced, more or less on the lines indicated in [the umbrella example], and distinguished publishers have not perceived that to offer to the public, with the sanction of their name, works of this sterilising and injurious character, is an offence against society. The body of a child is sacred in the eye of the law, but his intellectual powers may be annihilated on such starvation diet as this, and nothing said! The worst of it is, both authors and publishers in every case act upon the fallacy that well intentioned effort is always excusable, if not praiseworthy. They do not perceive that no effort is permissible towards the education of children without an intelligent conception, both of children, and of what is meant by education. (*Home Education*, pp. 246–47)

Notice what Miss Mason said must influence our approach to composition: an intelligent conception of children and education. In other words, our two vital principles: *children are born persons* and *education is the science of relations*. At its foundation, composition is based upon a desire to communicate with others; with narration, students always have something to say.

A sixteen-year-old who has been narrating orally from the age of six and has transferred that ability into writing fluency will not become the college freshman who causes his professors to despair. Whatever faults his writing might possess, he will have something to say and will know how to express it on paper. If we have taught him well, his writing will be an expression of the virtues he has learned to care about, including the virtue of clear, correct communication.

Things to Remember about Teaching Composition

1. Composition is grounded in narration, which begins with oral work.
2. The stages of narration build composition skills naturally.
3. Formal writing instruction can wait until a child is fluent in written narration.

Language: English Grammar and Foreign Languages

He has learned nearly all the grammar that is necessary when he knows that when we speak we use sentences and that a sentence makes sense.

Grammar Testifies to an Ordered Universe

The grammar of a language—even our native language—is quite an abstract concept, as it concerns the functions of words within a sentence and their relationships to each other. Historically, grammar as a liberal art included everything that would fall into the category we call literature, but even in its narrower sense of syntax and usage, grammar in the traditional trivium was a university-level study. Miss Mason found it difficult to teach grammar to young children, and that is why she suggested beginning with the basic concept of understanding what a sentence is:

> The class should learn,—Words put together so as to make sense form a sentence. A sentence has two parts, that which we speak of and what we say about it. That which we speak of is the subject.
>
> Children will probably be slow to receive this first lesson in abstract knowledge, and we must remember that knowledge in this sort is difficult and uncongenial. (*Philosophy of Education*, p. 210)

This very primary and fundamental approach to grammar is rooted in the principle that we live in an ordered and meaningful universe. In *The Liberal Arts Tradition*, Nietzsche is quoted as saying, "I fear we are not getting rid of God because we still believe in Grammar" (Clark and Jain, p. 36). Miss Mason would have understood that perfectly because she believed grammar was essentially grounded in the idea that a sentence makes *sense*. The order—the *logos*—of language implies meaning. Chaos and nonsense happen by chance, but order must be created. The uniformity of grammatical functions in every language is a testimony to the Creator of order in the universe. A noun is a noun in any language.

In practice, Miss Mason taught grammar slowly and systematically, but her fundamental concern was for children to grasp the meaning of using words in a sentence to make sense. She allowed children plenty of time to build their understanding of what a sentence is and how it is ordered before moving on to teaching parts of speech.

Languages Are Learned for the Sake of Communication

Like every other subject, the question of foreign languages is driven by the primary principles that *children are born persons* and *education is the science of relations*. Learning a language is a special way of developing a relationship with a people and a culture that would otherwise remain at a distance.

Miss Mason recommended French as a first foreign language because it was the obvious choice for English children to learn the language of England's nearest neighbor. She recommended other European languages for the same sort of reason—travel on the continent was common, and to be able to communicate or read in foreign languages was a great advantage. Americans are notoriously poor at teaching and learning foreign languages because we have few occasions to use them. English is the language of business and tourism, so our need for other languages is minimized, although the average European usually acquires proficiency in at least a second language, if not a third.

If we want to achieve something similar to what Miss Mason had in mind for foreign languages, we must look for the ways that such proficiency is possible. Most American programs do not aim at teaching students to speak and understand in the languages they study, so an examination of the methods Miss Mason recommended is very much in order.

Language Study Is Grounded in Communication and Relationship

The first lessons were conducted orally. Miss Mason assumed that the languages would be taught by those who were already fluent, which puts most of us at a disadvantage, but it is an incredibly effective method. My personal experience with learning a foreign language in the European style began with a small class of five or six students. No two of us shared the same nationality or first language. Besides myself, I remember a French woman, a Dutch woman, and a Japanese man. They all possessed the ability to communicate with me in English, which was also a foreign language for them, but the class was conducted in one language only, and that was Polish. I remember being stunned by the first hour-long lesson in a language that I simply did not know. We were expected to speak and answer in that language from the very first day. That was the key—I heard the words first, and I had to repeat them. I wasn't even sure what I was saying, but meaning gradually emerged as we each took our turn saying "My name is_____" in answer to the question "What is your name?" And we went on from there.

This common European practice is not unlike Miss Mason's methods for language. She began with oral practice and encouraged students to speak from the very beginning. Narration was used in the foreign language as well—children would be expected to narrate in the language they were learning.

> Young children find little difficulty in using French vocables, but at this stage the teacher should with the children's help translate the little passage which is to be narrated, then re-read it in French and require the children to narrate it. This they do after a time surprisingly well, and the act of narrating gives them some command of French phrases as far as they go, much more so than if they learnt the little passage off by heart. (*Philosophy of Education*, p. 211)

Miss Mason included Latin in language studies, but her focus was always on the relationship-building nature of what was being learned. Through Latin, students had the opportunity to develop a relationship with the people who lived in Ancient Rome.

> [Tommy] has to translate, for example,—*"Pueri formosos equos vident."* [The boys see handsome horses.] He is a ruminant animal, and has been told something about that strong Roman people whose speech is now brought before him. How their boys catch hold of him! How he gloats over their horses! The Latin Grammar is not mere words to Tommy, or rather Tommy knows, as we have forgotten, that the epithet "mere" is the very last to apply to words. Of course it is only now and then that a notion catches the small boy, but when it does catch, it works wonders, and does more for his education than years of grind. (*School Education*, p. 163)

In languages, as in all subjects, our educational efforts should be focused on building relationships.

Choosing a Language to Study Involves Relationships

The biggest question most modern educators have about foreign languages is "Which one?" Rather than prescribe, I would encourage you to remember the principle that *education is the science of relations*. Are there people you could communicate with if you spoke the language that they speak? Consider learning that language, not least because you can probably find a fluent speaker to help you in the process. If there is no one near you who speaks another language, choose one that you want to learn because you hope to speak or read in that language—reading is a form of communication too. Being able to read books in another language is a relational practice. Sometimes Americans want to learn a language that reflects their cultural heritage, and that is a kind of relation as well.

Once you have chosen, you will be faced with the task of finding curriculum and resources to help you learn, but we live in a world where that is possible. Computers, apps, and the internet even give us access to native speakers to listen to when there are none nearby.

Miss Mason urged two or three foreign languages on her pupils, and she had good reasons that correspond to the principles but are not demanded by them. The principles do not require that every person study multiple languages. Her students did not always reach full fluency in the languages they studied, but a smattering of German or Italian might let them communicate when they traveled, and reading in the languages was always an object. Consider your own needs and choose a language, perhaps two, but do not feel pressured to learn an arbitrary number of languages. Because *education is the science of relations*, your individual desire for relationships should govern the language or languages you choose to learn, as I chose Polish because I lived in Poland.

Things to Remember about Teaching Languages

1. Language—grammar and communication—are a reflection of an ordered universe. There is no such thing as "mere" words.
2. Hearing and speaking come before reading or grammar, and the best curriculum is a teacher fluent in the desired language.
3. Learning a language is a way of expanding our relationships with people and cultures.

Art and Music

There must be some reverent knowledge
of what has been produced.

Appreciation of the Arts

Charlotte Mason applied the same principle to the study of art as to everything else. *Education is the science of relations*, and the purpose of studying art is not to be able to explain techniques or styles. Rather, students should read paintings as they read books, spending some time with a painting as if it were a chapter and with several paintings from one artist as if he had a story to tell. This is picture study, as I described it earlier, and it is one of the easiest areas in which to see how education as the science of relations builds layers of relations over time.

> Children should learn pictures, line by line, group by group, by reading, not books, but pictures themselves. A friendly pic-ture-dealer supplies us with half a dozen beautiful little repro-

ductions of the work of some single artist, term by term. After a
short story of the artist's life and a few sympathetic words about
his trees or his skies, his river-paths or his figures, the little pictures are studied one at a time; that is, children learn, not merely
to see a picture but *to look at it*, taking in every detail. (*Philosophy
of Education*, p. 214)

A child forms a relationship with each picture he views and narrates. During the course of looking at several paintings from the
same artist, he builds a relationship with that artist. After meeting
many artists, he will begin to notice things, such as that some artists
paint with bright colors, while others seem to always use a darker
palette. Some artists paint with big, bold strokes, while other use
tiny brushes to create minute details. In this way, he will develop a
relationship with styles of art. Still later, his wider reading will bring
him to the place where he learns that the various styles of art represent ways of thinking and are expressions of worldview and ideas.
Truth, goodness, and beauty are particularly accessible in both art
and music.

The simple method of looking at a painting then describing it with
narration, which takes only a few minutes, is the foundation for a
well-developed appreciation of art that many adults might envy.

The same method is used with music. Our first object is exposure
to pieces or excerpts—often enough so that they become familiar.
Just as we focus on one artist at a time, becoming familiar with his
style and subject matter, we also listen to one composer at a time. Our
access to recorded music makes this study easier for us than it was
during Miss Mason's lifetime.

In her book *A Touch of the Infinite*, Megan Hoyt explores many of the
ways Miss Mason's principles can be used for music, and she reminds
us that music, like all the other areas of knowledge, comes from God.
Art and music, too, form a child's conscience and give him material
to inspire him and shape his character.

> Music is more than merely the backdrop of all these living ideas
> we are now slowing down long enough to ponder. It can be the
> vehicle with which we impress them upon our children, not in a
> rote way but naturally, over time. Music is the essence of inspira-
> tion itself; it is proof positive of the existence of God. (Hoyt, p. 23)

Participation in the Arts

In addition to appreciation of fine art and music, Miss Mason wanted students to take a hand for themselves. She wanted them to draw, paint, sing, and play an instrument as well if instruction was available to them. The children were not expected to reach professional standards but to train their eyes, hands, ears, and voices as best they could for the sake of delighting in drawing or singing. Because children are persons, they should have the opportunity to enrich their lives by developing relationships with art and music.

Things to Remember about Teaching Art and Music

1. Art and music are for everyone.
2. Children should look at paintings and listen to music just as they read books—to gain knowledge and ideas and to form relationships.
3. Children should learn to enjoy drawing and singing for themselves.

13

Daily Bread: Knowledge of the Universe

All classes must be educated and sit down to these things of the
mind as they do to their daily bread.
—Charlotte Mason, *A Philosophy of Education*

The two primary principles inform our approach to the knowledge of the physical world just as they do to all areas of knowledge. We are persons who need to develop relationships, including relations to the world that we live in. Knowledge of the universe is equivalent to natural philosophy, and it includes the study of things we can perceive with our senses.

In the modern world, we approach science from a very utilitarian stance. We want to know what it is possible to do, and we want to figure out how to do it. That knowledge represents power, and it has been the dominant approach since the Enlightenment. Prior to that, when people studied "natural philosophy" rather than "science," they looked at the world and marveled. The things that man was able to do were merely imitations of nature. Charlotte Mason's approach to knowledge of the universe belongs to that earlier tradition, when wonder and wisdom made the study of the natural world one avenue of learning to know God.

Science

The wonder of the world be ever fresh before [our] eyes.

Science Should Be Based in Reverence

One of the finest things Miss Mason did for education was to express the manner in which science should be approached as a liberal art. Therefore, like all the arts, it begins in wonder with wisdom as its object. Miss Mason encouraged reverent observation of natural things. She believed that every flower or tree is "a beautiful thought of God" (*Home Education*, p. 80), and that the natural world was full of common miracles for a child to discover. This fundamental relationship of the universe to God places science on a different footing than it is commonly understood.

Miss Mason's approach to science is grounded in the fundamental order of the world—a universe with a Creator who has created order and laws, and when any one of those laws is discovered, it is because God has revealed it. The life and laws of the natural world should inspire reverence.

> Reverence for *life*, as a wonderful and awful gift, which a ruthless child may destroy but never can restore, is a lesson of first importance to the child. (*Home Education*, pp. 62–63)

When this reverence is established, it will inform even the more clinical and analytical work that students might do later in their studies. During the elementary school years, at least, a child's study of science should be devoted to observing, recording, and learning to appreciate—to building relationships with the natural world. If we succeed in adhering to the twentieth principle by allowing no separation to grow in children's minds between this kind of knowledge and other knowledge of God, they will be able to approach more destructive kinds of experiments—such as dissection—from a posture of reverence. Miss Mason explained:

> Years hence, when the children are old enough to understand that science itself is in a sense sacred and demands some sacrifices, all the "common information" they have been gathering until then, and the habits of observation they have acquired, will form

a capital groundwork for a scientific education. In the meantime, let them *consider* the lilies of the field and the fowls of the air. (*Home Education*, p. 63)

There is a lovely moment in *A Girl of the Limberlost* by Gene Stratton-Porter when one of the characters expresses this sense of growing close to God because of an encounter with nature:

"There never was a moment in my life," she said, "when I felt so in the Presence, as I do now. I feel as if the Almighty were so real, and so near, that I could reach out and touch Him, as I could this wonderful work of His, if I dared. I feel like saying to Him: 'To the extent of my brain power I realize Your presence, and all it is in me to comprehend of Your power. Help me to learn, even this late, the lessons of Your wonderful creations.'" (Stratton-Porter, p. 297)

Nature Study Is the Gateway to Science

With such a lofty purpose to inform our approach to the universe, it is a relief to find that the actual practice of it is as simple as "consider the lilies of the field." Children begin this grand acquaintance with the universe by simply noticing whatever happens to be near enough for observation. Relationships begin at home. Are there six or seven trees along the street or in the back of the yard or easily within reach at the park? It would be a shame not to know the names of those trees, to recognize which ones will flower first in the spring or lose their leaves in the fall. Bark, twig, branch formation—we should recognize our tree neighbors by these as easily as we can identify them by leaf shape. A child who knows six or seven trees well has the foundation of a healthy knowledge of dendrology that will probably inspire interest in different trees he might see elsewhere.

When we fully apprehend the principle that *education is the science of relations*, we will perceive that it is not only a privilege but also a duty to pay attention to the natural world. That seems like strong language. Do we have a duty, an obligation to look at nature? Miss Mason thought so, and there are Scriptural injunctions to "go to the ant" (Proverbs 6:6) or "consider the ravens" (Luke 12:24). When the Bible says that a wise man will be like a tree (Psalm 1), it will mean little to us if we don't really understand trees.

But while we observe the trees, we will also be noticing the flowers, the insects, the birds, the weather, the geological formations, or the bodies of water within reach as well. This does not need to be overwhelming. We are not observing for the sake of a test or examination but for the sake of forming relationships with the world. The key is to open our eyes and look and to be sure that our children are doing the same. We keep on looking at things until the relationships form naturally, without pressure.

This is accomplished by simply spending time outdoors and learning to pay attention to whatever there is to see. In her PNEU programs, Miss Mason scheduled nature walks—at least once a week—and the children kept nature notebooks. Those notebooks were very personal. The children were encouraged to draw what they saw—both careful detail of a plant or creature and also more general impressions—a tree from a distance or the shape of a hillside. They were encouraged to keep lists of the flowers and birds they saw and to include bits of poetry that illustrated the season. The poetry was very important because the nature notebook at this stage is not a scientist's notebook with mere data but a relationship-building tool that increases a child's attention to what he is drawing and recording. It is meant to bring the child pleasure, and that delight is the basis of wonder and relationship—the beginning, so to speak, of wisdom. Miss Mason observed:

> Where science does not teach a child to wonder and admire it has perhaps no educative value. (*Philosophy of Education*, p. 224)

This is real knowledge—knowledge that a child gets for himself. This kind of firsthand knowledge lays a strong foundation for science because this is the raw matter of science itself—the natural world. A child who learns to draw a flower rather than tear it apart or, if it is picked, to put it carefully in water to keep it fresh as long as possible is laying a foundation of wonder and love and care for the natural world.

This is science as it ought to be begun, and we can supplement it by reading lovely, literary books written by naturalists who also love and care for the things they write about. I know a girl who devoured *Life a Spider* by Jean Henri Fabre and, after taking a close look and personal interest in those eight-legged arachnids, has never killed a spider since.

Relationship Governs Every Kind of Science

But what of more technological science—things like engines and robotics? The principle that *education is the science of relations* does not abandon these fields of knowledge or cease to operate when computers are introduced. I remember reading a lovely book about simple machines with my son when he was five or six years old. We performed easy experiments to demonstrate friction (rub your hands together quickly and feel the heat) and inclined planes. Early observation of these things is another way of forming a relationship with our world. Building with interlocking bricks is a kind of early engineering. Most children take delight in any kind of scientific knowledge that falls in their way, and there is no reason a child cannot have a relationship with robotics. Computer programming is all about logical, sequential *relationships*. All of these things can have a place in an educational paradigm governed by the principle that *education is the science of relations.*

One thing Miss Mason wanted teachers to remember is that the broad, vital principles of science are the living ideas that really matter—not the experiment or cute trick. Scientific demonstrations should not seem like magic or illusions but should be linked to genuine appreciation for the natural laws of the universe:

> The utility of scientific discoveries does not appeal to the best that is in us, though it makes a pretty urgent and general appeal to our lower avidities. But the fault is not in science...but in our presentation of it by means of facts and figures and demonstrations that mean no more to the general audience than the point demonstrated, never showing the wonder and magnificent reach of the law unfolded. (*Philosophy of Education*, p. 318)

The principle of a wide and generous curriculum means that, in the later years, students will address botany, biology, chemistry, astronomy, and any number of other scientific disciplines. The early foundation of wonder and delight in the natural world means that these studies will not be dry and lifeless for them because they have a context and meaning with which they are already familiar. Science does not have to be utilitarian:

> "I think that is very wonderful," a little girl wrote in an examination paper after trying to explain why a leaf is green. That little girl had found the principle—admiration, wonder—which makes science vital, and without wonder her highest value is, not spiritual, but utilitarian. (*Philosophy of Education*, p. 317)

Maintaining a sense of wonder and relationship is the most important thing we can do as we learn science. Knowledge of the world is part of the living, vital knowledge that a person wants to know—one aspect of wisdom. Because all knowledge has the same source, the study of science is a glimpse into the mind of God.

Things to Remember about Teaching Science

1. Observation should be rooted in wonder.
2. Children should observe the things immediately available to them and keep a nature notebook to foster their relationships.
3. Scientific pursuits should be accompanied by reverence for God, not treated as something separate.

Geography

When I heard of any new kingdom beyond the seas, the light and
glory of it entered into me.
—Thomas Traherne, quoted by Charlotte Mason

Observe Your Local Geography

Although we might think of maps at the first mention of geography, and maps certainly do have their role, we need to pause for a moment and recollect that this falls under the heading of natural philosophy, or knowledge of the world. Maps may be of two kinds. There are physical maps that show the natural features of the land—rivers, mountains, and bodies of water—and there are political maps that show the boundaries of various countries or states. Learning political maps is certainly a valid pursuit, and we are sometimes chagrined by our own shortcomings in this area of knowledge.

Have maps and a globe readily at hand. It is an excellent practice to make a habit of locating the different places you read about or places that are in the news. If you are reading *Heidi*, you should discover where Switzerland lies. If you hear that the Olympics will be in Beijing, you should find out exactly where that city is located. Miss Mason included a few minutes of map work in her school schedule each week, which allowed children to become familiar with the continents, countries, cities, and seas.

But political maps are not the only concern of geography. This aspect of knowledge of the universe is about the natural world, and many of the things that fell under the heading of geography when Miss Mason wrote about it seem more like aspects of science to us— things like the relationship of the sun and the earth in the various seasons, latitude and longitude, the observation of geological formations such as mountain ranges and river basins, and the operations of tides.

Nevertheless, that is a hint that our approach to geography should be much like nature study. All that has been said about science applies to geography as well. We want to get out and see what is available to be seen—to notice and to think. There is a creek nearby. Where does it begin and where does it go? We should be able to see what effect it has had on the land around it. Has a hill been cut away to make a way for a road? Can you see layers of rock in the cutaway? Do they lie at an angle? Let us wonder. How did they come to be that way? Hills, mountains, ponds, the seaside, the swamp, the desert— you live somewhere, and wherever you live, there is a geography to be observed, and that is where you and your children can begin to develop your relationship with geography.

Read about Faraway Places

We are also intrigued by other places that are extremely different from our own. If we live on a plain, the mountains are a breathtaking wonder. If we live in the mountains, the seaside is an inexpressible delight. I spent most of my early life in the lush, humid eastern states, and my first visit to the Sonoran Desert awakened an enduring love for that beautiful arid place.

Most of us travel only a little, so our opportunities to see the geography of the world are limited. Miss Mason urged us to let children experience that geography through the eyes of those who did travel, who had their eyes open and alert and wrote about their experiences for others. If you are not likely to make a trip around the Mediterranean Sea, you can travel there vicariously by reading the account of a person who did.

Miss Mason included a warning in some of her comments about geography that is well worth remembering. We aren't learning about geography, or anything else, for the sake of showing off or feeling superior. Knowledge is for the sake of relationships, and if what we learn doesn't make us care about the things we are learning about, it has no lasting value. When we choose books, we want to choose ones that have the flavor of a relationship, not mere information.

> The so-called scientific method of teaching geography now in vogue is calculated to place a child in a somewhat priggish relation to Mother Earth; it is impossible, too, that the human intelligence should assimilate the sentences one meets with in many books for children, but the memory retains them and the child is put in the false attitude of one who offers pseudo-knowledge. (*Philosophy of Education*, pp. 339–40)

The principle that *education is the science of relations* means that you do not have to learn "*all* about anything"—that is part of the twelfth principle—but that you set out to form relationships with the things that are in your reach, which includes both the things you can observe and the things you can read about.

Things to Remember about Teaching Geography

1. Have maps and a globe on hand for both study and frequent reference.
2. Become acquainted with the geography of your neighborhood and places you are able to visit.
3. Read books that will allow you travel vicariously to places you may not be able to see for yourself.

Mathematics

We take strong ground when we appeal to
the beauty and truth of Mathematics.

Math Has a Beauty That We Should Appreciate

Miss Mason called mathematics a "mountainous land which pays the climber" (*Philosophy of Education*, p. 51). It gives us a lovely picture of deep valleys and steep, heavy climbs rewarded by enthralling vistas. While we would welcome more practical hints from her, she said comparatively little about the teaching of math because "it is receiving ample attention, and is rapidly becoming an instrument for living teaching in our schools" (*School Education*, p. 236). This is not necessarily true for us today, so we must glean as much as we can from what she has given us. As with all areas of the curriculum, *education is the science of relations* is the guiding principle.

Miss Mason included a caution not to allow mathematics to assume a disproportionately large place in the curriculum. This is tempting today because math is vital in science and technology, but that utilitarian view of math should not be our focus. There is always a risk of math assuming too large a role because it is so easy to test in math. Miss Mason urged us to look past these things and approach math with the same wonder we bring to nature or stories:

> But education should be a science of proportion, and any one subject that assumes undue importance does so at the expense of other subjects which a child's mind should deal with. Arithmetic, Mathematics, are exceedingly easy to examine upon and so long as education is regulated by examinations so long shall we have teaching, directed not to *awaken a sense of awe in contemplating a self-existing science*, but rather to secure exactness and ingenuity in the treatment of problems. (*Philosophy of Education*, p. 231, emphasis added)

She thought that the actual teaching of math depended greatly on the teacher, but she gave us some guidelines for the wisest approach to take. Math taught for the sake of just finding the correct answer to a problem is math taught far below the level that it should be. Memorizing formulas and computational tricks is not really mathematical thinking. Math is full of relationships and laws of the universe. An appreciation of that concept is the soundest foundation for teaching math.

> From this point of view, of immutable law, children should approach Mathematics;...The behaviour of figures and lines is like the fall of an apple, fixed by immutable laws, and it is a great thing to begin to see these laws even in their lowliest application. The child whose approaches to Arithmetic are so many discoveries of the laws which regulate number will not divide fifteen pence among five people and give them each sixpence or ninepence; "which is absurd" will convict him, and in time he will perceive that "answers" are not purely arbitrary but are to be come at by a little boy's reason. Mathematics are delightful to the mind of man which revels in the perception of law, which may even go forth guessing at a new law until it discover that law. (*Philosophy of Education*, p. 152)

Computation Should Be Based on Relationships

Education is the science of relations in math as in everything else, and nowhere more than in the laws of number are patterns and relationships so observable. How many is one? A contemplation of "oneness" could occupy a lifetime. What happens to one when a second one is added? And another one? And another one? You can also spend time contemplating "twoness" and "threeness" and "four-ness." Suppose you examine all the numbers from one to ten very carefully. There is a great deal to think about. Besides the differences between oneness and twoness and sevenness, you can divide your numbers between those that can be lined up in pairs (even numbers) and those that cannot (odd numbers). You can ponder the rationale and logic for the way that ten is written (10), what place value means, and why we have only ten digits (including zero). You can wonder if it's possible to come to the end of numbers or if you can keep adding one forever. If you have blocks and you make a "staircase" with the even numbers and another one with the odd numbers, the "steps" are the same size—and you can ponder the reason for that.

These are fairly simple ideas, all of which can be explored in kindergarten, but we have a tendency to ignore the ideas in math and focus on computation rather than relationships. Miss Mason cautioned us: Don't do that. Develop a relationship with arithmetic that is based on understanding the relationships that are in arithmetic.

Geometry and algebra are nothing but a description of relationships that exist.

There is a very good chance that you never had the opportunity to think of math in this way and never developed a relationship with it yourself. It is important to realize that you cannot give what you do not have, and if you want your child to experience math in a relational way, you might have to spend some time doing that yourself. I'm unfamiliar with the most current math curricula available, but one older program that encourages the kind of play and exploration that allows mathematical relations to emerge and creates opportunities for children to discover them for themselves is Miquon Math. With the use of Cuisenaire rods, it lays a foundation for mathematical comprehension and provides a glimpse of the vistas math offers.

Miss Mason was opposed to using "rods and staves"—manipulatives—for doing computation once a child understood the principles at work, but that is not a prohibition against using them at an earlier level of mathematical exploration, when the idea of number and computation is still abstract. Miss Mason wanted children to understand the principles, the "whys" that lie behind mathematical computation, rather than just learning by rote. You can use pebbles or buttons to prove to yourself that three groups of six make eighteen things altogether rather than merely parroting "3 x 6 = 18."

When you are choosing a math curriculum, I would encourage you to keep the principles in mind—*children are born persons* and *education is the science of relations*. You will be best served by a math program that respects your child's personhood and thinking mind and offers a relational approach, rather than a mechanical one, to teaching number concepts. Within arithmetic, a child will meet some of the most elegant laws of the universe, and a program that enables him to retain wonder and awe as he learns is more desirable than one that hurries him through computation.

Things to Remember about Teaching Mathematics

1. Math is based in absolute laws of the universe.
2. You can discover and understand those laws, which are about relationships.
3. Computation will be most successful when it is based on understanding mathematical principles.

Physical Education and Handicrafts

The divine Author of your being has given you life, and a body
finely adapted for His service; He gives you the work of preserving
this body in health, nourishing it in strength, and training it in
fitness for whatever special work He may give you to do
in His world.

Relationships with Activity

Under the heading of knowledge of the universe, Miss Mason
included all the things that we can do physically. These, she told
us, do not properly fall under the heading of education, which is
primarily for the spiritual mind, but rather training. She made the
distinction clear:

> Physical and mechanical training are necessary for the up-bring-
> ing of the young, but let us regard them for the moment as train-
> ing rather than education,—which ought to concern itself with
> things of the mind. (*Philosophy of Education*, p. 255)

Nevertheless, because children are relationship-building persons,
there is a whole realm of dynamic relationships for them to develop:

> There are, what I may call, *dynamic* relations to be established. He
> must stand and walk and run and jump with ease and grace. He
> must skate and swim and ride and drive, dance and row and sail
> a boat. He should be able to make free with his mother earth and
> to do whatever the principle of gravitation will allow. This is an
> elemental relationship for the lack of which nothing compensates.
>
> Another elemental relationship, which every child should be
> taught and encouraged to set up, is that of power over material.
> Every child makes sand castles, mud-pies, paper boats, and he
> or she should go on to work in clay, wood, brass, iron, leather,
> dress-stuffs, food-stuffs, furnishing-stuffs. He should be able to
> make with his hands and should take delight in making. (*School
> Education*, pp. 79–80)

Because these relationships are also important to cultivate, Miss
Mason included things like drill—a kind of exercise program—into
the school day. She had mixed feelings about sports and games
because there are more important things to think about than having

fun. She wanted to be sure that children understood the reason behind physical health and fitness—so that they would be in fit condition for whatever service they might be called to do:

> The object of athletics and gymnastics should be kept steadily to the front; enjoyment is good by the way, but is not the end; the end is the preparation of a body, available from crown to toe, for whatever behest "the gods" may lay upon us. (*School Education*, p. 102)

Cultivating good habits for exercise and physical fitness will pay lifelong dividends, and Miss Mason considered this a duty—one of the things that a person who lives in an ordered universe should not fail to do.

Relationships with Materials

Besides physical fitness, Miss Mason wanted children to learn to work with the raw materials of clay, wool, leather, or wood to make things that were beautiful and useful. She considered things like the joining of wood as ideas inspired by God.

> This is the history of every great invention and every great discovery of the secrets of Nature. "Then David gave to Solomon his son...the pattern of all that he had by the spirit, of the courts of the house of the Lord." We have here a suggestion of the source of every conception of beauty to be expressed in forms of art. (*Parents and Children*, p. 272)

Handicrafts offer the opportunity to build habits of tidiness, perseverance, and carefulness. Miss Mason insisted that slipshod work should never be allowed and that these crafts produce worthwhile things. With *children are born persons* and *education is the science of relations* to guide us in this, as in all areas of the curriculum, we can ask what handicrafts have been taken up and pursued throughout history. The list is long enough to provide a choice that will suit everyone, and no one needs to attempt them all.

We might consider sewing, embroidery, knitting, crocheting, bobbin-lace making, wood turning, carving, leatherwork, scroll-saw work, origami, glassblowing, stone carving, clay modeling, tinwork, or weaving. Perhaps the arts of gardening, cookery, bread making and cake decorating also fall into this category as food is a raw material similar to wood, clay, or textiles.

Miss Mason told us about using paper sloyd (similar to origami) and clay modeling in her schools, as well as weaving and leatherwork. However, every kind of craft brings its unique enrichment to a child's experience. Which handicrafts we choose matters less than the manner in which we approach our work. Excellence is the standard because excellence in handiwork is something that a person can achieve. This is not about artistic talent but about learning to handle material and tools effectively because that is proper work for a person.

Things to Remember about Physical Activity and Handicrafts

1. Physical training of body and hands is an important aspect of personhood.
2. Physical fitness is a duty we owe ourselves and others whom we want to serve.
3. Whatever crafts we choose, we should strive to do them well.

Education Is the Science of Relations in All Things

This concludes our broad look at all the areas of a curriculum, although each of them can be considered in more detail than there is room for here. You can explore the more practical ways that Miss Mason taught each subject elsewhere, including the sources mentioned on page 114. Nevertheless, she assured us that education grows practically out of our understanding of ideas and philosophy.

She had absolute faith in the central principles of her paradigm—*children are born persons* and *education is the science of relations*. She knew that children need to develop relationships and that their proper food is living ideas. Because she was so certain, she was less concerned about perfect implementation than she was about keeping those principles at the forefront of our efforts. She urged:

> Let us try, *however imperfectly*, to make education a science of relationships—in other words, try in one subject or another to let the children work upon living ideas. In this field small efforts are honoured with great rewards, and we perceive that the education

we are giving exceeds all that we intended or imagined. (*School Education*, p. 163, emphasis added)

If you understand the central principles of her paradigm as well as the captain idea that governs each area of study, you will discover that your efforts, *however imperfect*, will yield more than you thought possible. Children are not clay to be molded so that the results depend on our own skills. Rather, they are persons who will grow and develop naturally so long as they are properly fed. Miss Mason wanted us to understand that spreading a feast of knowledge is something we are fully able to do. Our children will take what they need and will be nourished. They will learn, and they will grow.

14

In a Nutshell

Great ideas are brooding over the chaos of our thought.
—Charlotte Mason, *Parents and Children*

In this final chapter, I want to offer a concise overview of the way that the principles operate together to form a body of cohesive thought, along with a graphic representation of their relationship. I hope that this will solidify all that I've said before, but I also hope it will serve in the future as a quick reference to refresh your thoughts about the principles. Remember that the principles you know, understand, and embrace as your own will guide your actions the way your knowledge that "water flows" or "gravity pulls" governs your behavior. When you know these principles as well as you know those truths, your teaching endeavors will be safeguarded from the educational equivalent of leaping from the top of a roof. You simply will not implement practices that violate the principles.

There Are Two Central Principles

As we have seen, two primary principles lie at the heart of Charlotte Mason's educational philosophy. Like the blossoms on a flower, they should be the first thing that catches our eye—the bright, fragrant truths that arrest our attention. The first is *children are born persons*. A person is a spiritual being, not merely physical, and our educational efforts must address that spiritual nature while also caring for the child's physical well-being. He is not a machine to be programmed or an animal to be trained. He is a person with a mind and a heart who has tendencies that must be nurtured or restrained, and it is the work of the educator to oversee and direct his moral development.

> But the educator has to deal with a self-acting, self-developing being, and his business is to guide, and assist in, the production of the latent good in that being, the dissipation of the latent evil, the preparation of the child to take his place in the world *at his best*, with every capacity for good that is in him developed into a power. (*Home Education*, p. 9)

The second vital truth is *education is the science of relations*. All the knowledge in the world is intimately linked through its common source, the Holy Spirit. This great recognition means that each person is meant to form relationships with knowledge in every realm of reality—the knowledge of God, the knowledge of man, and the knowledge of the universe. The formation of those relationships, along with a steadily growing perception of the relationships that "bind all things to all other things" (*Parents and Children*, p. 259), is the process of education at its best. It is the process by which a person develops wisdom and virtue, so that he may indeed become that best that it is possible for him to be.

The Central Principles Are Related to Each Other

These two primary principles intersect with each other to give us the concept of a person forming a relationship with all that it means to be a person. *Know thyself.* In order to know yourself so that you can best govern yourself, you must know all the possibilities that lie within all persons. The two most vital things to understand about a person—the things that set him apart from all other beings—are the nature of the *will* and of *reason*. Using our wills and making intelligent and virtuous choices is the distinctive work of a person. The nineteenth principle explains:

> Therefore, children should be taught, as they become mature enough to understand such teaching, that the chief responsibility which rests on them *as persons* is the acceptance or rejection of ideas. To help them in this choice we give them principles of conduct, and a wide range of the knowledge fitted to them. (*Philosophy of Education*, p. xxxi)

One of the things I've saved for this final chapter is Miss Mason's own philosophy in a nutshell in which she addresses these primary, vital truths. She recognized that this blend of the two primary principles encompassed the idea of "knowing thyself:"

> "Man, know thyself," is a counsel which we might render, "Child, know thyself, and thy relations to God and man and nature." (*School Education*, p. 118)

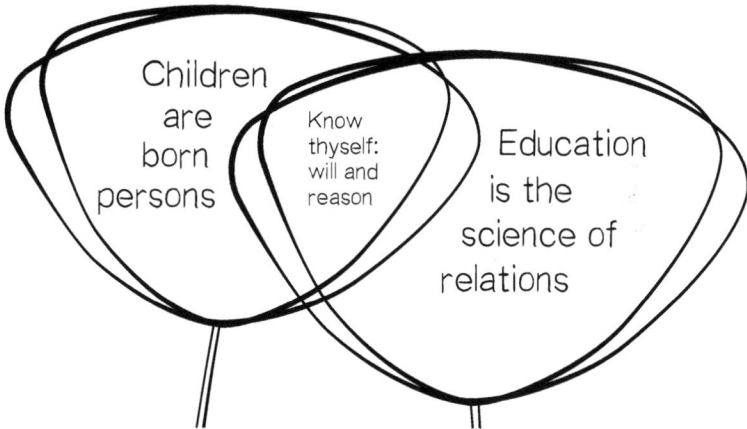

She followed this summary with an admonition for parents:

> To give their children this sort of preparation for life it is necessary that parents should know something of the laws of mind and of the source of knowledge. (*School Education*, p. 118)

Everything else that is a part of this educational philosophy works in vital harmony with this central idea: "Know thyself, and thy relations to God and man and nature." We must understand the principles, which are laws of nature, that are at work in this process. Our task as educators is to encourage children to blossom in virtue and character, and we will have the most success when we work "upon lines of law which go to the producing of a human being at his best" (*Home Education*, p. 5).

The Central Principles Have Several Adjunct Principles

Once we are well-acquainted with the blossoms of our flower and have fully appreciated them, we can examine the philosophy-plant more closely. When we do, we will find some leaves—adjunct principles—attached to the primary ones. The principle that *education is the science of relations* is enhanced by the idea that we should not allow any *separation* between things spiritual and things intellectual. There is only one source of knowledge, and mathematical or grammatical truths have the same divine origin as things we label "religious." If our educational work is relationship-driven, we don't want to allow any kind of separation—the opposite of relationship—in our approach to knowledge:

> But it would be well if we could hinder in our children's minds the rise of a wall of separation between things sacred and things so-called secular, by making them feel that all "sound learning," as well as all "religious instruction," falls within the office of God, the Holy Spirit, the supreme educator of mankind. (*School Education*, p. 146)

The primary principle that *children are born persons* is illuminated by making several observations about persons and their place in the world. They do not have natural or preprogrammed characters. Because they are not simply born good or born bad, the work of educators, both parents and teachers, is to nurture them—to set their feet on the right paths and help them develop a virtuous life, which should not be conflated with the work of salvation from sin. The task of education is necessary because we live in an ordered universe governed by moral authority that has given us a standard of virtue to aspire to. Moral authority has shown us that there are things we ought or ought not to do and has laid a duty upon us to strive for that virtue. Because we are persons endowed with reason and will, we can both understand what is right and then choose to act rightly. These ideas are ensconced in the PNEU school motto: "I am, I can, I ought, I will."

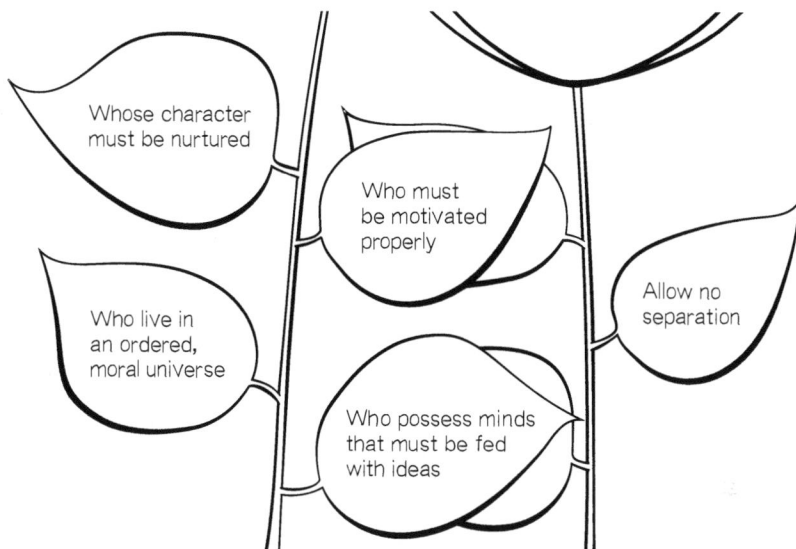

Whose character
must be nurtured

Who must
be motivated
properly

Who live in
an ordered,
moral universe

Allow no
separation

Who possess minds
that must be fed
with ideas

A few of the leaves overlap a bit, and we can see that because children are persons who will be forming many vital relationships, we must be sure we motivate them properly. We should not allow unlawful motivations, such as fear, into our educational efforts. It is also possible to lean too heavily on legitimate motivations, such as the desire for rewards (grades, prizes, scholarships) in a way that stifles the natural motivation of a person to learn—the natural hunger to know. Wrong motivation in education may hinder the healthy growth of relationships, and it may weaken the will of the student.

As educators, we too are under authority, and we are not free to employ any means whatsoever as we teach. Remembering the principles that *children are born persons* and *education is the science of relations* will give us courage to let their natural desire to know develop without artificial or external pressure.

Because children are persons, they do have minds that are hungry for knowledge. They are born with a desire to form relationships with all the wide realm of things that it is possible to know. To feed them well, the relational provisions we offer them must be generous. They will only be able to form all the relationships that are proper and possible for them if we remember that they will grow and form on *ideas*. Their spiritual minds must be nourished with proper food.

Mere information will not satisfy their hunger, but ideas will shape their consciences and inspire right habits.

Practical Principles Make the Philosophy Work

Finally, in the roots of our plant, we will find the more practical aspects of a Charlotte Mason education—the things that will keep the whole harmonious unity alive and flourishing.

Within our roots we will find those three instruments of education allowed to us: an atmosphere, a discipline, and a life. These are the things we can legitimately use to educate a person. Exposure to life and our place in it—home, church, and community—creates an atmosphere that educates children without direct effort. However, our effort *is* needed to help them develop the habits—physical and intellectual—that will support them in living a virtuous life. We are creatures of habit, and if we do not take care to form good habits, bad habits establish themselves instead. Finally, we are reminded again that ideas are the food upon which a person must live and thrive. Education is a life—a right understanding of education does not restrict learning to certain places or ages. Everywhere we go, any time of day, and throughout our whole lives, living persons should be learning persons. These three things—atmosphere, discipline, and life—are the paths we take to teach our children their duty in the world.

The most practical principles Miss Mason gave us for academic education can be summed up by saying that students must read and narrate many living books. Those books must include a great variety of knowledge—literature, history, philosophy, science—because they have to sustain all the various relationships and also provide children with the moral knowledge they will need to help them *will* right choices.

> Children are not to be fed morally like young pigeons with pre-digested food. They must pick and eat for themselves and they do so from the conduct of others which they hear of or perceive. But they want a great quantity of the sort of food whose issue is conduct, and that is why poetry, history, romance, geography, travel, biography, science and sums must all be pressed into service. No one can tell what particular morsel a child will select

for his sustenance. One small boy of eight may come down late because "I was meditating upon Plato and couldn't fasten my buttons," and another may find his meat in "Peter Pan"! But all children must read widely, and know what they have read, for the nourishment of their complex nature. (*Philosophy of Education*, p. 59)

The lovely blossoms and the leaves that embrace and enhance them may charm us, but if our plant is a living plant, it must also have roots. Cut off from the roots, the blossoms and leaves will remain fresh for only a short while before they wither and fade. To remain strong and living, there must be roots through which the life-giving nutrients—the inspiring ideas of truth, goodness, and beauty—may flow.

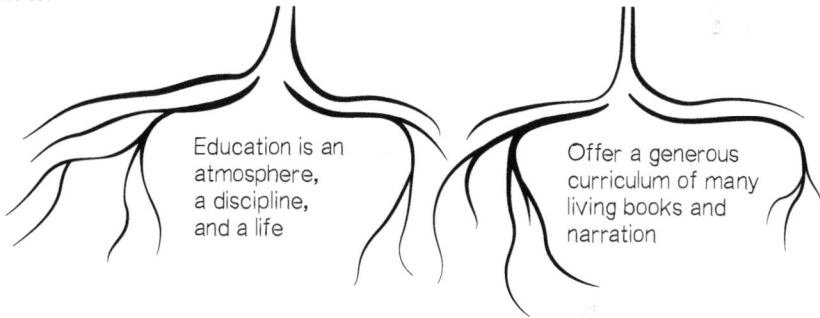

Education is an atmosphere, a discipline, and a life

Offer a generous curriculum of many living books and narration

This Harmonious Philosophy Is for Everyone

I hope you will read through the principles as Miss Mason presented them to us, which I have included in the appendix. I hope you will read at least one, if not more, of the volumes she wrote to elaborate on her ideas. But don't forget the essential unity of the principles as you explore the various details of this philosophy and its methods.

The twenty principles—several parts working together in vital harmony—represent a living force in education. Because the ideas in these principles are grounded in the laws of the universe, they operate in every aspect of our lives with the same force as the law of gravity. Miss Mason reminded us that "if Tommy drops his spoon, it falls to the ground," and that, too, is a law of God (*School Education*, p. 129). We cannot ignore the physical laws of the universe, and when we shape our actions in accordance with them, we are able to make use of them in mighty ways.

It is the same with these laws of education. Children are born persons, and if you teach them as persons should be taught, you will enable them to form the relationships that will enhance their lives and motivate them to live virtuously. Their own experience will be rich and rewarding, but like a blooming flower, they will also bring a bit of beauty, color, and fragrance into each life they touch. If we could educate many such persons, the world might resemble a garden.

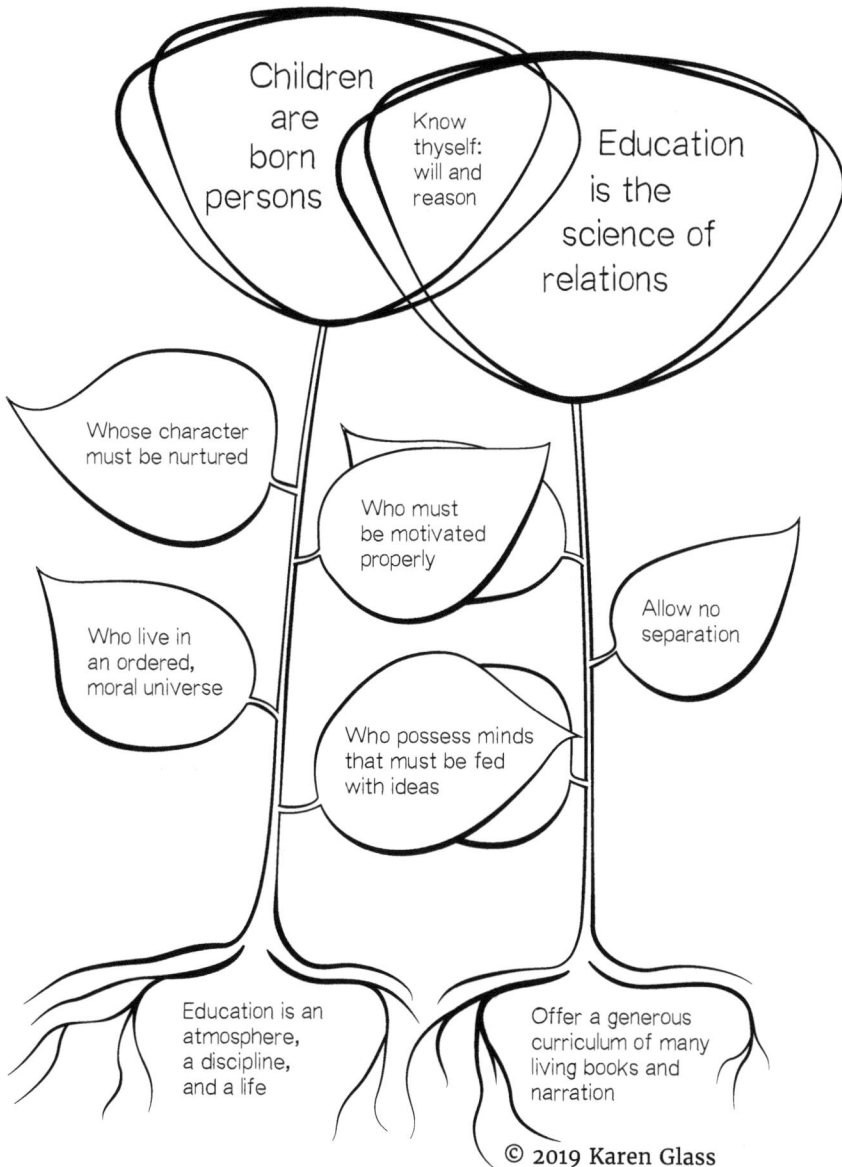

Children are born persons

Know thyself: will and reason

Education is the science of relations

Whose character must be nurtured

Who must be motivated properly

Allow no separation

Who live in an ordered, moral universe

Who possess minds that must be fed with ideas

Education is an atmosphere, a discipline, and a life

Offer a generous curriculum of many living books and narration

© 2019 Karen Glass

Appendix: Charlotte Mason's Educational Principles

1. Children are born *persons*.

2. They are not born either good or bad, but with possibilities for good and for evil.

3. The principles of authority on the one hand, and of obedience on the other, are natural, necessary and fundamental; but—

4. These principles are limited by the respect due to the personality of children, which must not be encroached upon whether by the direct use of fear or love, suggestion or influence, or by undue play upon any one natural desire.

5. Therefore, we are limited to three educational instruments—the atmosphere of environment, the discipline of habit, and the presentation of living ideas. The P.N.E.U. Motto is: "Education is an atmosphere, a discipline, and a life."

6. When we say that *"education is an atmosphere,"* we do not mean that a child should be isolated in what may be called a "child-environment" especially adapted and prepared, but that we should take into account the educational value of his natural home atmosphere, both as regards persons and things, and should let him live freely among his proper conditions. It stultifies a child to bring down his world to the child's level.

7. By *"education is a discipline,"* we mean the discipline of habits, formed definitely and thoughtfully, whether habits of mind or body. Physiologists tell us of the adaptation of brain structures to habitual lines of thought, *i.e.*, to our habits.

8. In saying that *"education is a life,"* the need of intellectual and moral as well as of physical sustenance is implied. The mind feeds on ideas, and therefore children should have a generous curriculum.

9. We hold that the child's mind is no mere sac to hold ideas; but is rather, if the figure may be allowed, a spiritual organism, with an appetite for all knowledge. This is its proper diet, with which it is prepared to deal; and which it can digest and assimilate as the body does foodstuffs.

10. Such a doctrine as *e.g.* the Herbartian, that the mind is a receptacle, lays the stress of education (the preparation of knowledge in enticing morsels duly ordered) upon the teacher. Children taught on this principle are in danger of receiving much teaching with little knowledge; and the teacher's axiom is, "what a child learns matters less than how he learns it."

11. But we, believing that the normal child has powers of mind which fit him to deal with all knowledge proper to him, give him a full and generous curriculum; taking care only that all knowledge offered him is vital, that is, that facts are not presented without their informing ideas. Out of this conception comes our principle that,—

12. *"Education is the Science of Relations,"* that is, that a child has natural relations with a vast number of things and thoughts: so we train him upon physical exercises, nature lore, handicrafts, science and art, and upon many living books, for we know that our business is not to teach him all about anything, but to help him to make valid as many as may be of—

"Those first-born affinities
That fit our new existence to existing things."

13. In devising a *syllabus* for a normal child, of whatever social class, three points must be considered:
   (a) He requires *much* knowledge, for the mind needs sufficient food as much as does the body.
   (b) The knowledge should be various, for sameness in mental diet does not create appetite (*i.e.*, curiosity)
   (c) Knowledge should be communicated in well-chosen language, because his attention responds naturally to what is conveyed in literary form.

14. As knowledge is not assimilated until it is reproduced, children should "tell back" after a single reading or hearing: or should write on some part of what they have read.

15. A *single reading* is insisted on, because children have naturally great power of attention; but this force is dissipated by the re-reading of passages, and also, by questioning, summarising, and the like.

Acting upon these and some other points in the behaviour of mind, we find that the *educability of children is enormously greater than has hitherto been supposed*, and is but little dependent on such circumstances as heredity and environment.

Nor is the accuracy of this statement limited to clever children or to children of the educated classes: thousands of children in Elementary Schools respond freely to this method, which is based on the *behaviour of mind*.

16. There are two guides to moral and intellectual self-management to offer to children, which we may call "the way of the will" and "the way of the reason."

17. *The way of the will*: Children should be taught, (a) to distinguish between "I want" and "I will." (b) That the way to will effectively is to turn our thoughts from that which we desire but do not will. (c) That the best way to turn our thoughts is to think of or do some quite different thing, entertaining or interesting. (d) That after a little rest in this way, the will returns to its work with new vigour. (This adjunct of the will is familiar to us as *diversion*, whose office it is to ease us for a time from will effort, that we may "will" again with added power. The use of *suggestion* as an aid to the will is *to be deprecated*, as tending to stultify and stereotype character. It would seem that spontaneity is a condition of development, and that human nature needs the discipline of failure as well as of success.)

18. *The way of reason*: We teach children, too, not to "lean (too confidently) to their own understanding"; because the function of reason is to give logical demonstration (a) of mathematical truth, (b) of an initial idea, accepted by the will. In the former case, reason is, practically, an infallible guide, but in the latter, it is not always a safe one; for, whether that idea be right or wrong, reason will confirm it by irrefragable proofs.

19. Therefore, children should be taught, as they become mature enough to understand such teaching, that the chief responsibility which rests on them *as persons* is the acceptance or rejection of ideas. To help them in this choice we give them principles of conduct, and a wide range of the knowledge fitted to them. These principles should save children from some of the loose thinking and heedless action which cause most of us to live at a lower level than we need.

20. We allow no separation to grow up between the intellectual and "spiritual" life of children, but teach them that the Divine Spirit has constant access to their spirits, and is their Continual Helper in all the interests, duties and joys of life.

Bibliography of Works Cited

Augustine. 426 AD. *On Christian Doctrine*. Christian Classics Ethereal Library. http://www.ccel.org/ccel/augustine/doctrine.

Bestvater, Laurie. *The Living Page: Keeping Notebooks with Charlotte Mason*. N.p.: Underpinnings Press, 2013.

Cholmondeley, Essex. *The Story of Charlotte Mason (1824–1923)*. 2nd ed. Petersfield, UK: Child Light, 2000.

Clark, Kevin and Ravi Scott Jain. *The Liberal Arts Tradition: A Philosophy of Christian Classical Education*. Camp Hill, PA: Classical Academic Press, 2013.

Glass, Karen. *Know and Tell: The Art of Narration*. N.p.: Karen Glass, 2018.

Hoyt, Megan. *A Touch of the Infinite*. N.p.: Powerhouse Press, 2016.

Mason, Charlotte M. *Formation of Character*. 1905. Reprint, Wheaton, IL: Tyndale House, 1989.

———. *Home Education*. 1886. Reprint, Wheaton, IL: Tyndale House, 1989.

———. *Ourselves*. 1904. Reprint, Wheaton, IL: Tyndale House, 1989.

———. Parents and Children. 1904. Reprint, Wheaton, IL: Tyndale House, 1989.

———. *A Philosophy of Education*. 1925. Reprint, Wheaton, IL: Tyndale House, 1989.

———. *School Education*. 1904. Reprint, Wheaton, IL: Tyndale House, 1989.

Montaigne, Michel de. "Of the Education of Children." In *Essays of Michel de Montaigne*, translated by Charles Cotton and edited by William Carew Hazlitt. 1877. Project Gutenberg, 2006. http://www.gutenberg.org/files/3600/3600-h/3600-h.htm.

Muir, John. *My First Summer in the Sierra*. Boston and New York: Houghton Mifflin Company, 1917.

Parents' National Educational Union. *In Memoriam*. London: PNEU, 1923.

"Parents' Review School." *The Parents' Review* 12, no. 9 (1901): 968–70.

Plato. *Laws*. Translated by Benjamin Jowett. 1871. Project Gutenberg, 2008. https://www.gutenberg.org/files/1750/1750-h/1750-h.htm.

Rooper, Thomas Godolphin. *Educational Studies and Addresses*. Glasgow and Dublin: Blackie and Sons, Limited, 1902.

Ruskin, John. *The Crown of Wild Olive*. Edited by J. H. Fowler. London: MacMillan and Co., Limited, 1921.

Stratton-Porter, Gene. *A Girl of the Limberlost*. Bloomington and Indianapolis: Indiana University Press, 1984. First published 1909 by Grosset and Dunlap.

White, Anne E. *Minds More Awake: The Vision of Charlotte Mason*. N.p.: Anne White, 2015.

Quintilian, Marcus Fabius. *Quintilian on Education: Being a Translation of Selected Passages from the Institutio Oratoria*. Edited and translated by William M. Smail. New York: Teacher's College Press, 1966. First published 1938 by Oxford University Press.

Printed in Great Britain
by Amazon

36444241R00104